PADDY'S PEOPLE

PADDY
O'GORMAN

POOLBEG

Published 1997
by Poolbeg Press Ltd
123 Baldoyle Industrial Estate
Dublin 13, Ireland

© Paddy O'Gorman 1997

The moral right of the authors has been asserted.

A catalogue record for this book is available from the British Library.

ISBN 1 85371 351 1

Cover photography by Michael Edwards
Cover design by Poolbeg Group Services Ltd
Set by Poolbeg Group Services Ltd in Garamond 10/14
Printed by The Guernsey Press Ltd,
Vale, Guernsey, Channel Islands.

ABOUT THE AUTHOR

Since 1984 Paddy O'Gorman has had remarkable success and popularity as a broadcaster and journalist. He is well-known for his RTE radio programme *Queueing for a Living*. His book based on the radio programme, *Queueing for a Living,* became an instant bestseller.

CONTENTS

Chapter One

CRUSTIES: THE HIPPIES OF WEST CORK

The Bogfield, near Dunmanway;
August 1994

Deirdre and I went hippy-hunting in West Cork. It was Sunday and I needed material for my show the next morning on RTE Radio Cork. The RTE jeep was handy for the hills and muddy boreens. We searched everywhere. Ballydehob, Clonakilty, Dunmanway. We found a lot of respectable English alternative-lifestyle types in the craft shops – metal workers, basket-makers, artists and the like – but I wanted the unrespectable ones. The crusties. The unwashed ones with long, matted hair, ragged clothes and working-class English accents. Living in Cork city over the last couple of months, I had seen a lot of crusties. Sometimes they pulled up in their old vans and buses overnight at Union Quay, just outside the RTE studios. But they were just passing through. I was in West Cork now because I wanted to find where the crusties were nesting.

In Dunmanway we were told about the Bogfield at Coolmountain, a few miles outside town. We got lost. We saw a fairly new-looking car parked, facing away from us on the grass verge by the roadside. We pulled up alongside and asked the man in the driving seat for directions. He was aged about forty and had a local accent. He seemed to get a fright. He only barely opened his window and wanted to get rid of us as quick as he could. You want the third mountain on the left.

I drove on. I was laughing at the vagueness of the directions. Deirdre was laughing, too, and her face was flushed. Did I not notice what that guy was doing? No, I didn't. From the passenger side of the jeep, Deirdre had a clear view down at the fellow. He was wanking. You serious? Imagine the shock he got when he saw an RTE van bearing down on him. No wonder he wanted to get rid of us.

We continued our hippy-hunt. Which is the third mountain on the left? We followed a boreen for some miles, then came upon what we were looking for.

There were fifty or more dwellings that I could see in the Bogfield. There were old vans and buses, caravans and tents, shanties and dome-shaped constructions that I learned were called benders. It was a cold, rainy day, like most of the days in the summer of 1994 and most of the dwellings had smoke coming from them. There were dogs and a few horses around but the place looked different to an Irish travellers' site (I mean travellers in the sense that we used to call tinkers). There was no washing hanging out. No waste plastic or metal lying around. The caravans were generally small and old and looked as if they would fall apart if they were towed too roughly. Even the poorest Irish traveller has a better caravan to live in.

We parked at the edge of the field, conspicuous in the RTE jeep. We were next to a big old van with three crusties sitting outside it. The van was a heavy, dark green vehicle that looked like something from maybe the 1950s. Vans of that vintage seem to be particularly prized by the crusties.

The Bogfield was muddy underfoot. The three crusties, two men and a woman, watched us with suspicion, if not outright hostility, as we came near. I said hello. I made no attempt to hide my tape-recorder and microphone. On a job like this you have to be upfront with people. I decided to walk past these three. At the next caravan there was a woman of about twenty-five. She was fat, sallow-skinned, maybe of Asian background and very pretty. What counted most was that she smiled as we said hello. I stopped to talk.

Her name was Sarah. She had a friendly, working-class London accent. She had three children and had been living here since May. There's two of the children over there, she said.

I looked at the children and got a shock, then checked my reaction so that Sarah wouldn't notice. I looked at Deirdre. Her jaw had dropped and her face was full of concern and disbelief.

The children were naked, playing among the brambles on what was a cold, wet, windy day. Close your mouth, Deirdre, I thought. Don't let Sarah see that look on your face. It's perfectly normal to have your children out naked on a day like this. Sure, wouldn't we all send our kids out like that?

Please close your mouth, Deirdre. I need to get material on tape and if I want to get people to talk, I can't let them get the impression that I don't approve of them. Sarah was the only hippy we had met so far who was being friendly and I didn't want to waste her. I caught Deirdre's eye and pressed my finger under my jaw. Deirdre copped on and closed her mouth.

(Since that day, I have learned from other Cork people

that crusties commonly let their children out naked. It's their way.)

Up close, I could see Sarah had rivulets of mud caked on her neck. I guess the rivulet pattern is caused by the action of sweat on dirt. Like most crusties, she had a sort of sheen of dirt on her skin. I think the expression "crusty", which I learned in Cork city, probably refers to that crust of dirt on these people's skins. They themselves like to be called travellers, hippies or new-agers. They probably don't like being called crusties but, to me, crusties is the most evocative and descriptive name for them.

I have a baby, too, said Sarah. And do you look after the children by yourself, Sarah? No, Dee lives here with me.

Sarah pointed to the caravan and through the door to where Dee sat cradling the baby. What was I looking at? My brain reacted against what I was seeing. It took a few moments to make sense of it all.

Dee, like most crusties, had long, matted hair. In Dee's case, the hair was so matted and dirty it was like the contents of an old horse-hair mattress. It gave the impression that it was moving by itself. But maybe if I describe Dee from the feet upwards you will understand my initial mental confusion at what I saw.

Dee wore big, Wellington boots under a knee-length, flouncy blue dress. Tugged around the shoulders was a granny-type white cardigan, buttoned up at the front. All Dee's visible skin, except for the face, was covered in intricate, blue ink tattoos. The neck tattoo was like a Celtic collar with zoomorphic designs. Dee was big, with broad shoulders straining out from under that dress and buttoned-up cardigan. The face was tough and weathered-looking with a strong jaw and bristly chin. Dee was a man of about forty-five.

Dee was friendly and pleased to talk. His accent was Geordie.

I like it here. I can live how I want. I don't waste my time on brushing my hair. It's against my religion. 'Ippy people accept me as I am. Some people don't accept me because of the way I dress, you know?

Yes, Dee, I was going to ask you about that. You dress in an unusual way?

I wear the female clothes, you know? I'm a transvestite. I'm not queer. (He said the word with emphasis. KWEE-ah.) This is me and Sarah's baby here. I didn't like Cork cos people called out names at me on the street. I've been beat up. But 'ippy people here in Bogfield accept me. People don't look at you twice.

(I could imagine the names Dee got called by the youngsters in the streets of Cork. He didn't have to convince me about that.)

Sarah told us they planned to turn the caravan into a tattoo studio for Dee to work from and make money. Good idea, I said. I hope it works.

(Holy Jesus. A tattoo studio. What about hygiene? I barely felt safe shaking hands with Dee, never mind having him stick a needle in my skin.)

The baby looked up calmly, safely cradled in his dad's lap. I wondered what age that child would be when he began to notice that his dad looked unusual and not like other dads. I suppose the child would be older still, and taunted by other children, by the time his dad's bizarre appearance might begin to bother him.

I looked around the caravan. It was small, old and wooden. The floor was broken and falling away at one corner, causing a draught. The bed was a large wooden shelf built across one end and taking up about half the caravan space. All five of them slept on that bench. A wood-burning stove smoked away near the door. They collected the fuel locally in the fields and forests.

We said goodbye to Dee and Sarah. I squeezed Deirdre's hand and made small talk as we walked away from the caravan. Deirdre understood me. Let's not talk yet. We'll have plenty time to talk later.

We met Alan, who was about twenty. He was tall with long hair and spoke in a moaning, effeminate, working-class London voice. I was reminded of a Monty Python character who used to use a voice like Alan's.

Alan told us he lived in a teepee. He slept on a bed of reeds because he liked to be close to the earth. He had lived in a caravan and didn't like it because it wasn't close enough to the earth. He was from Tottenham and was a drug addict there. He used to get depressed living in his flat in a tower block. Now he no longer took heroin. Here he had only the odd bit of what he called pipe. That's hashish.

Alan liked the older Irish people. He had an 'orse here in the Bogfield. That's something that older Irish people understood. He liked talking to old farmers who had 'orses too. He had a lot in common with older Irish people because they were still close to the earth like he was. He didn't have much in common with the younger Irish, who were too materialistic.

Alan was nice. He seemed a gentle, friendly person. So what if he had funny notions about the supposed lack of materialism on the part of older Irish farmers? At least here he was away from heroin. There's no heroin in Cork so Alan was safe. Perhaps some day he would get sick of living in a teepee and would become more materialistic. In the meantime, anything was better than heroin addiction.

I asked Alan about his teepee. He pointed to it at the far end of the field. It was, as its name suggested, a thing like you'd see in an old cowboy and Indian movie. It had a single long branch up through the middle surrounded by a canvas sheet pulled around in a conical shape. It was just about wide enough at the base for a man to lie down in but it must have been cramped, cold and dark in there. Soon he was going to build a bender because the bender would be better in the Irish climate. Other people live in benders, said Alan. His friend Aurora lives in a bender. Would we like to see?

We crossed a ditch to the next field. Aurora's bender was in the shelter of a wall and a few trees. It was built up against the side of a small caravan. The bender was of an elongated dome shape, covered in tarpaulin. Alan lifted one of the sheets of tarpaulin. This was the door. There was nobody in, but he brought us in to sit down.

The bender was constructed from a frame of interwoven holly branches. The frame was supported by a number of strong wooden branches from other, less flexible types of trees. The floor was made of sheets of plywood which, I guess, were recovered from dumps and skips. The floor was springy underfoot and was supported, I expect, by large stones that kept it raised above the damp ground of the Bogfield. At one end of the room, sheets of clear plastic were used instead of tarpaulin, giving the effect of a living-room's bay windows.

There was a three-piece suite of furniture. We sat on the couch. I wondered about insect-infestation. Think about all the earwigs you get in the folds of a deck chair if it's left out for even a couple of nights. This couch must have been crawling, but at least it was dry.

Some vegetables were hung from the ceiling. There was

a basket full of ornaments made of beads, small painted stones for hanging around your neck and lanyard bracelets in the process of being woven. (I remember learning to weave lanyards among the hippies of Charlsfort, Kinsale back in 1973 when I was sixteen. This new generation of hippies had some things in common with the hippies of a generation before and lanyard-weaving was one of them.) In the corner of the bender there was a wood-burning stove that was smoking. Aurora hadn't gone too far.

A few minutes later, Aurora came back in. She was a stout young woman with short-cropped hair and a strong, cheerful, Manchester voice. She had a high colour in her cheeks from the wind and the rain that was now falling. She carried a basket of vegetables that she had just bought from a local farmer. I can't remember the exact price she paid, but I remember Deirdre saying to her that she had got lovely vegetables at a good price. Aurora said that she always buys locally rather than walking miles into town to pay a higher price.

Aurora seemed pleased to have visitors. Alan told her who we were and she didn't stop smiling. Good. Then two men came in. They were carrying wood for the stove. One was a young man who didn't talk much. The other was a Londoner. I didn't like the Londoner from the start.

He was in his early thirties. He told us he used to work in the Middle East for £1000 a week but had given it up to live as a traveller. He didn't smile. He wanted to know what we were trying to achieve with this radio show. The media completely misunderstands people like him. The Londoner was all attitude, challenging me every chance he got.

I had no interest in interviewing the Londoner but I was interested in Aurora and I knew that the Londoner was going to make that difficult. I recognized the Londoner as the sort of man who can be handled by flattery if he can't be got rid of. And as I was on his territory here, getting rid of him wasn't going to be practical. It had to be flattery.

Please, can you explain to me this lack of understanding that the media suffers from? Please tell me. People like me need to know.

You wouldn't understand, he said. The Londoner refused to be interviewed on tape, just as I had hoped and expected.

A woman came in with a baby. Aurora smiled and took the child. This was her baby, aged nine months. The baby was born here in the Bogfield last November. Are you serious? Can you tell me about that please, Aurora?

She was born into water. We made a pool in here in the bender. I'd seen it done before. We got two doors from a lorry and hung a sheet of like thick, black plastic stuff between them. Then outside we heated the water on a fire and eh . . . it was a lot of water. We got one of those milk tanks that the farmers have to take their quota of milk to the dairy. So we built a fire and heated that outside. That was a hundred gallons of water which was boiling. There was already cold water in the pool inside and we brought in buckets . . . while I was in labour there was a stream of people walking past me with buckets of hot water. (Aurora was laughing here.) And they poured it in on me and it was hot. It was very hot. I was only in it fifteen minutes and she came out. Yeah. It was really wonderful.

Were you worried in case there was any complications during the birth? Did you have a midwife with you?

Yeah. I had a professional midwife. I wasn't worried. My last birth was at home, too. That was a dry birth but I thought the birth into water was, for me, really wonderful.

I knew this was a remarkable story. It's a story I have often been asked about since by people who heard it on the radio. Aurora's wasn't the first birth in the Bogfield so it wasn't so remarkable to her and her hippy friends but, to the rest of us, it was extraordinary. I could see my own look of wonder reflected in Deirdre's face. Women would love this story, too. It was the sort of thing you see in women's magazines. I gave birth in a wet, windy, West Cork field in a plastic sheet hung up between two car doors and surrounded by hippies who poured buckets of hot water in on me. Brilliant stuff.

There was still the problem of the Londoner with attitude, glowering in the corner. Your questions are really ignorant, he said. Typical media. You don't understand that birth is a completely natural process. A woman doesn't need pain killers and all those other things that are just the interventions of western medicine. You don't realise quite how ignorant you are.

Okay, I said, perhaps you're right. Maybe there's a lot I don't understand. But I think I was asking the sort of questions that would occur to most men and women who would be listening to Aurora's story and who don't look at childbirth in the way that you do.

I was polite to the Londoner, but now I had what I wanted on tape so I was finished kissing his ass. Putting up with the Londoner had been part of the price of getting the interview with Aurora and, as far as I was concerned, it had been a price worth paying. But he wasn't finished yet.

You need to talk to somebody who really knows something about an alternative, new-age lifestyle. Somebody who gave up well-paid work to live like this. But you need to know what questions to ask, not your ignorant questions. Like you were talking to Dee and Sarah. They don't have a clue. You need to talk to somebody like me but I wouldn't be willing to talk to you unless you asked the right questions and you need to learn what the right questions are.

This guy had another think coming if he thought I was going to sit around being lectured by him to end up with some boring, rambling nonsense on tape about alternative lifestyles. No, I really feel I need to learn a lot more before I could interview somebody like you. There was no irony in my voice but I think he got the message. He could beg me all he liked but I wasn't budging.

Aurora offered us tea. Thank you, that would be nice. I have a policy of accepting tea while working no matter where I am. It's polite. Alan said he would get milk. He came back a minute later with a half-full milk bottle. I guess it was got from a local farmer. Aurora boiled water on the wood burner. Aurora enjoyed chatting and extending hospitality to her guests. When the tea came, the mugs weren't very clean but the taste was good.

I asked Aurora about rent. The farmer charged £3 per dwelling per week in the Bogfield and the price went up for the settlements higher up Coolmountain. I thought about that. I reckoned that meant the farmer was getting up to £200 a week in rent from the Bogfield alone. No wonder the crusties were tolerated here.

Is it cheaper anywhere else? Not any more, said Aurora. The farmers were undercutting each other for a while but had come up with an agreed rate for all around West Cork.

Why more expensive up Coolmountain? The farmer there

charges more, said Aurora, because the people have more money. They're snobs up there. They have posh accents. One of them was a television producer before he came here. They have fences around their houses and won't let people like us go up there.

I nodded in understanding. I had heard of new-agers with posh English accents signing on at the dole in the police station in Dunmanway. But all the ones here in the Bogfield had working-class accents. Everybody was supposed to be adopting an alternative, non-materialist lifestyle but, even here in Arcadia, there was class distinction.

I asked where the toilet was. Alan directed me to a ditch surrounded by brambles. When I got there it was disgusting. There was human waste and also the place doubled as a refuse dump. There were egg shells, potato peels and so on. At least there were no plastics dumped there. The lifestyle of the Bogfield didn't tend to produce plastic waste. But the smell of shit was awful and I think it was a safe bet that there were rats around attracted by the refuse. I didn't jump down into that ditch. I would wait until I found a toilet somewhere else.

Back at the bender, Aurora had a small transistor radio. I tuned it to where I hoped she would get RTE Radio Cork the next morning. Out of curiosity, I asked if they ever watched TV. To my surprise they said yes. There were some tellies in the Bogfield in caravans with generators and, during the World Cup over the previous few weeks, a telly had been set up in a tent in the middle of the field for everyone to watch.

Deirdre and I shook hands with Aurora and the others and thanked them for their hospitality. We walked back out among the benders and caravans and towards our jeep. Okay, Deirdre. Just keep smiling until we're out of sight. We got into our jeep and headed away. We both let out a deep breath. At last we could talk freely and give vent to our feelings about what we had seen. We had feelings of shock, hilarity, incredulity and a lot else besides.

We headed to Cork city. When we got there we went to a nice restaurant and had wine. We were a million miles now from the Bogfield and all its discomfort. Jaysus, did you ever see anything like it? said Deirdre, doing her salt-of-the-earth, working-class Dub thing that irritates me sometimes but that I was enjoying now. When we saw Dee, I didn't know if I was looking at the granny, the auntie or what. And Alan in his teepee. He's close to the earth all right. When he went out for the milk I had a vision of him catching a goat somewhere. And what about Aurora in her birthing pool? Ah, yeah. Let everybody in the field come along with their bucket of water and see your fanny. No thanks.

We talked, too, about the local farmers and the money they made from renting land to the crusties. One farmer to another surveying the fields: a fine crop of hippies you have there, Mick. And what about the rent price war between farmers that had now been settled? Hippy-poaching, I suppose you'd call it.

And what of the crusties themselves? Why do they do it? Most are from poor backgrounds to begin with, but they have chosen a lifestyle that is poorer still. The hippies of a generation before were largely of middle-class background. Drop out, tune in, turn on and all that. The new-agers we met that day had dropped out, for the most part, only from English dole queues and gone to Irish ones instead. They had very little to drop out from in the first place.

We left the restaurant and headed for my flat on Wellington Road. The weather had turned wet and very windy now. We thought about what it must be like down in the Bogfield. We were glad of our warm bed.

Chapter Two

Some Stories that Never Were

The Crying Virgin of Neilstown
Neilstown Estate, Clondalkin, Dublin;
September 1994

A statue of the Virgin Mary, in a church in the Neilstown area of Dublin, was reported to be crying. It made news for a few days and crowds turned up. After a few more days, interest faded and the statue didn't cry any more.

Now I can tell you that the virgin's tears were made of Windolene. I hope the man who since told me the real story won't be cross at me for repeating here something he told me one night over a pint. He's a priest. He and I have been friends for some time and I hope our friendship will survive his reading this.

What really happened with the statue was that one of the cleaning staff was using Windolene and somebody else thought the stuff was tears. I'm not sure whether or not this was a deliberate hoax by the cleaner. Anyhow, some of the worshippers in the church decided that they saw the statue crying, they ran into the sacristy to tell the priest, the priest declared it to be a miracle and, a few days later, he used a television broadcast of Mass from that church to pass on the news to the nation.

A couple of days after the story broke, I went to Neilstown presbytery to report on the crying virgin phenomenon for RTE's *Today at Five* programme. When I got there, the priest who had announced the story was not available for comment. I expect he was, by then, being held incommunicado in some special room in the Archbishop's house. So I spoke with my friend, the priest whom I knew. He wouldn't comment on the crying statue but he made me welcome, along with Deirdre who was with me that day.

Neilstown, my friend's parish, is one of the poorest places in Ireland. We talked about drugs and unemployment. My friend was obviously more comfortable dealing with worldly problems rather than with miracles. At times, I wonder about his faith. He seems unsure about life after death. Religion is all about how you live this life, Paddy, he tells me.

Outside, at the church, people were arriving looking for the miracle. A nun was meeting them, trying to talk the thing up. She was middle-aged and had a rural accent. Isn't it great that Our Lady has come to Neilstown? We must listen to Our Lady's message which is to pray. The nun showed none of my friend's embarrassment at the story. If the Archbishop had already issued a diktat to shut up about the whole thing, it didn't seem to have reached that nun.

Deirdre and I went in to look at the statue. It was a typical, sad-eyed, painted Virgin Mary. There were no tears. There wasn't a huge crowd in the church, just a steady trickle of the faithful and the hopeful. People were saying rosaries, looking to the statue for another outbreak of crying.

There weren't many cars outside so I guess the congregation was made up mainly of locals. But I saw one woman who didn't look local. It wasn't just that she was too well-dressed. It was that she didn't have the hard, worn look of the local people. Poverty leaves its mark on a person's face and gait. Generations of poverty make people look like they do in Neilstown.

The well-dressed woman stayed standing as she looked at the statue, softly mouthing prayers. She was in her late thirties. She had two small children with her. She had a sick pallor but she still had better skin than most of the local women of the same age. Fewer lines. Probably a non-smoker. She wore a scarf around her head. There was something unusual about her eyes but I didn't quite take in at the time what it was. She was crying as she persisted in her quiet imploring of the Virgin Mary. I had seen enough. I touched Deirdre's arm. Let's go.

Outside, Deirdre asked me if I had noticed the woman with the head-scarf who was crying. Yes, I did. But did I notice her eyes? Yes, there was something unusual, I said. What was it? Deirdre told me. She had no eyebrows.

Deirdre has seen cancer in her own family and couldn't fail to recognise it now. The woman with no eyebrows was wearing the head-scarf to cover her baldness. She was on chemotherapy.

I felt sad and I felt angry. Sad is easy to explain. A young mother with cancer had come looking for a miracle. But why angry?

First, a word about miracles. I don't believe in them. People see miracles if they want to see them and the types of miracles that are seen are determined by the kind of people that see them. Take flying saucers. People have been seeing flying saucers for the last fifty years or so because, since the development of rocketry, the idea of interplanetary travel has been able to enter the popular imagination.

In the last century there were no flying saucers because

17

people couldn't imagine such a thing. In Victorian England, people used to report sightings of a fellow called Spring-Heeled Jack who would jump over houses and terrify people. Spring-Heeled Jack was about the most fantastic thing that people of that time could imagine.

Irish miracles involve the Virgin Mary. As the Catholic and nationalist development of Ireland gained momentum through the last century, the Virgin Mary became an increasingly important icon, almost like a public figure in Irish life. No wonder, then, that one afternoon the Virgin appeared in Mayo. It was only to be expected that she should visit a people who had come to love her so much.

The Virgin Mary appeared in Knock because people wanted her to appear. The statue of the Virgin was seen to be crying in Neilstown because people wanted to believe that it was crying.

I'm angry because a woman with cancer was given false hope. It was tragic for that woman to have cancer. But the priests and nuns couldn't leave bad enough alone. They made a fool of her, too.

The Drug Feud that Never Happened
Cork;
April 1995

Michael Crinion was shot dead outside a pub in Cork City on the evening of Saturday, April 8, 1995. It was widely reported in the newspapers that this killing was part of a feud between rival drug-dealing gangs in Cork and that more murders were to be expected. A few days later, I took the train to Cork to report on this supposed drug-feud for the *Pat Kenny Show*. During the train journey, I read the press cuttings that I had run off the RTE computer the previous day. These were articles on the Crinion murder and on other drug-related stories in Cork over the last few years. After a while of reading, before ever reaching Cork, I began to doubt the drug feud story.

Journalists affect all sorts of inside knowledge that they don't have. The most fanciful speculations are given weight by prefacing them with the claim that "gardai believe" a certain version of events to be true. I think the police sometimes entertain themselves by taking journalists aside and seeing how much they can get them to believe.

One newspaper said there was a feud going on over the heroin supply to Cork, not knowing that there is no heroin supply to Cork. Another paper, establishing a non-story that still turns up from time to time, linked the Crinion murder to the disappearance of three men who had all lived in the same flat on Wellington Road. The paper claimed that the three men in the flat were drug-dealers who were murdered by "a ruthless Mayfield drug gang" because they owed the gang money.

The Mayfield angle interested me. I know the drug scene in Mayfield and the Glen well from the time I worked in Cork for three months in 1994. I knew where the young people gathered to buy and to smoke their dope. I would probably be able to find the drug-dealers too. I decided that Mayfield would be my starting point in Cork.

It was a bright spring morning. When the train arrived in Cork station I decided to walk to Mayfield. It's a nice walk, across from the railway station and then up the steep steps and alleyways of Cork's northside. Walking gives me thinking time, too. Time to rehearse what I'm going to say when I'm at the front doors of people I haven't seen for some time. I mean, how do you ask people tactfully what they might know about a murder?

The housing in Mayfield is improving over the years, although some of the houses and inhabited blocks of flats are still among the worst dumps in Ireland. How do places get like that? Okay, the people themselves are to blame for a lot of the problems. They smash glass, piss on the stairways, scrawl graffiti on the walls and dump shitty nappies on the footpaths. But the housing itself is awful. You can smell the damp and mildew in places that were only built in the 1960s. The window-frames are rotten. The pre-fabricated walls are crumbling. Lots of the flats have been boarded up or abandoned to the young gangs of the night.

I headed for the home of the Mayfield person who was top of my mind. Helen's nice. She's someone I have got on with ever since I first met her in the housing queue at Cork City Hall in June of 1991. She doesn't do drugs but she spent time in Mountjoy in her younger days because of drink-related crime. She used to get violent when she drank and was convicted, as a teenager, for assaults against gardai and others. These days, in her late twenties, she seems so calm, it's hard to imagine her violent past.

I knocked at Helen's door. Here's hoping that she's in and that she'll be pleased to see me. Helen answered the door and hugged me. That was a good start. Her two little boys came out to say hello. I asked Helen about Peter, the man in her life when I last met her. She threw her eyes up. Oh, he's back inside through drink and robbing. He'll never grow up. She was with a different man these days.

I asked Helen if there were still drugs being dealt on the waste ground near her home. She was surprised by my question. There is of course, she said. They're there every evening around five o'clock. One local dealer was out of

Limerick prison in the last few weeks and was back in business. There were two other local men also dealing. And are they not frightened, Helen, by the southside gang that's supposed to be taking over the drug trade on the northside? Helen laughed. That was the first she'd heard of it but I would have to ask the dealers for myself. She would speak to them this evening. I'll tell them you're all right, Paddy, and ask them to talk to you. Come back this time tomorrow.

I spent the rest of the day looking up old contacts in Mayfield, the Glen and Knocknaheeny. I got to know these places over the years through standing outside the welfare offices and post offices of the northside, talking to anyone who would talk to me. I've built up a lot of addresses, a lot of houses where I can get a cup of coffee.

All day long, I got the same reaction whenever I asked people about Michael Crinion. Nobody mourned him. Cork was relieved that he was dead. He was violent to a psychopathic degree. Everyone had a horror story about him. One time he lacerated the face of an old man who looked at him the wrong way in a pub. People felt that Crinion got what was coming to him. Clearly, Cork's florists were experiencing no great demand for wreaths following the death of Michael Crinion.

So Crinion had few friends and lots of enemies. If he had been found beaten to death in an alleyway there would have been plenty of people as suspects. You can't go around beating people up and not expect to get a beating yourself sometime. But Crinion's murder appeared to be of the type that's called professional, that is, the work of a hired killer. It was carefully planned and carried out in a way that would leave the minimum of clues. (At the time of writing this, more than two years after the event, nobody has yet been charged with the murder of Michael Crinion.) My guess is that there was a falling out over money, which means it was more likely that Crinion's murder was paid for by one of his own business associates rather than by somebody from another gang.

That evening, I sat in a pub in town and watched the news on television. An RTE camera crew was attacked while filming Crinion's funeral. Both the cameraman and the sound man were seriously injured when they were thrown from the roof of a building from which they were filming. I got talking with other men in the pub. They told me about Crinion's associates, the southside gang that the newspapers called the Untouchables. Some were in prison in Ireland, one in England and one in Holland. They didn't sound untouchable to me. And yet we had politicians declaring that Cork's crime problem was out of control, that the police were ineffective and that new laws were needed to prevent the city being taken over by these untouchables. The pub consensus was that the untouchables were untouched by common sense. Tonight some of Crinion's pals were on television carrying out an assault. Really bright.

The next afternoon I called to Helen again. She had spoken with the dealers. The lads said that's okay, Paddy. They'll talk to you.

I walked to the area where the dealing takes place. It's on high ground overlooking the Northern Ring Road. All approach roads can be seen from the dealers' vantage point. Cork city was over the brow of the hill behind us. In front of us was the valley of the Glen and, beyond that, green fields stretched away to the north. A line of young men queued for the men who were obviously the dealers. One of the dealers, a man in his mid-twenties, was crossing off names on the back of a cigarette packet. He looked up when I approached with my microphone and he guessed who I was. He was friendly and cheerful. Come on over.

The dealer said to me that I was welcome to talk to his customers but that he didn't have much to say to me except that he hoped cannabis would never be legalised because if it was he wouldn't make so much money from selling it. I spoke to the customers and explained that I was looking for views on whether or not cannabis was harmful and whether or not it should be legalised.

The customers were all young men. They were here for £10 deals. That was the usual amount. Most, but not all of them, were unemployed. They get a supply of cannabis here maybe twice a week. Cannabis is a good drug, they said. Does you no harm and calms you down. It's cheaper than drink. We were in fierce trouble when we used to drink, fighting and all of that, but we're grand on drugs. You should try it.

(I still wonder why there were no women among the customers. It's something I can't easily explain although I'll have a go later.)

Young men kept appearing and getting their £10 deals. The deals are cut in thin strips about the length of your little finger. The strip is sealed tightly in silver paper. It looks to me like these prepared deals have been machine-cut and packaged. Not like the rough lumps of hash we used to get when I was a lad.

One of the dealers was an older man, about mid-thirties. He would say nothing for my microphone. He looked worried the whole time. He wasn't unfriendly, just cautious. He had just finished a spell in Limerick, he told me. The other dealer, the talkative one, decided he had things to say to me after all.

The guards never catch us cos if they come over they never find the stuff cos 'tis planked. Then if they find where 'tis planked, it's not ours. We know nothing about it. 'Tis like a wheel. There's three of us has it moving all the time. We never has enough on us for them to say we're dealing.

There's policemen watching us right now. There's a squad car stopped just outside Mayfield Shopping Centre down there. There's also a motorbike cop going around the housing estates behind us. Do they ever come over here and try to stop the dealing?

No. Sometimes they come in to my house and bring me down the station and annoy me head for hours asking me stupid questions and all. Then they leaves me go again.

What have you got written on the cigarette packet there?

I uses this to take fellahs' orders and to mark off who's paid me and who hasn't, like. Tonight's the night that most fellahs settle their accounts.

Do you sell just here in Mayfield?

I meets fellahs in town too if they want to place an order, like.

Anywhere you wouldn't sell?

The southside.

I pressed the dealers and their customers about a drug war in Cork and I soon began to feel silly. They hadn't a clue what I was on about. From reading the newspapers, you would have thought that all of Cork's northside was cowering in fear or, as one newspaper put it, "bracing themselves for the next hit". It wasn't like that. The drug-dealing here was relaxed and uneventful. Buying cannabis was as routine as any other type of shopping.

But I knew that I was taping something that, to most of my listeners, would seem anything but routine. RTE Radio One broadcasts to Middle Ireland. By Middle Ireland I mean people who respect the law, people who vote, people who lobby their TD if they feel strongly enough about something, people who keep a critical eye on the police or any other State body that they might suspect of being lax about doing its job. Middle Ireland is made up of people who take part in the democratic process.

My druggies in Cork were underclass people who aren't part of that process. They had barely heard of RTE Radio One or the *Pat Kenny Show* or any other programme. They had no understanding that what, to them, was the routine business of drug-dealing would sound profoundly shocking to the people of that other world that is Middle Ireland. I was feeling just a little bit guilty about taking advantage of my interviewees. They sensed that I didn't disapprove of them so they were friendly and willing to talk. But I knew that, by talking to me, these young men were unwittingly doing damage to the drug-dealing business in Mayfield.

I was about to leave when a man who was standing there watching asked to speak with me. He was in his late thirties and was out walking his dog when he came over to see what was going on. He waited patiently while I interviewed the dealers and their customers. When I finished taping, he asked me if I would come and meet someone who, he felt, was getting a bad time from the newspapers. I didn't know what to expect but I agreed to go with him. We walked to a nearby house where the man introduced me to a woman who was his friend. He was spending a lot of time with her these days, he told me, just to be with her during what was a stressful time in her life.

Jean Bailey was mid-thirties, attractive with long hair. She told me that she was the brother of "Patch" O'Driscoll, one of the three men who had gone missing from the flat in Wellington Road. She believed her young brother was murdered and his body buried somewhere but she didn't believe the newspaper story that he was murdered as part of a feud among drug-dealers. Her brother drank, she said. He was never a drug-dealer.

We spoke for an hour or more. I reassured her that I didn't believe the story about the Mayfield drug gang killing Patch. I didn't believe there was any drug war in Cork. I offered her the chance to speak on the phone to Pat Kenny on air the next day but she said she was happy to let me do the talking for her.

(I dread to think what Jean made of the newspaper story the following Sunday, that "gardai believe" that Patch O'Driscoll murdered his two flatmates and then was himself murdered by somebody else. There was no evidence produced by the journalist to support this most unlikely theory. But journalists know that you can't be done for libel if your victim is dead, so they could print any shite they wanted about Patch O'Driscoll. Open season on a dead man.)

Back in Dublin a few days later, I was on the *Pat Kenny Show* with my drug-dealing tapes from Cork. After the taped report went out, Pat interviewed me in studio. For Jean Bailey's sake, I passed on my view that the murder of Patch O'Driscoll was not drug-related. I had, by now, a statement from the gardai in Cork to help me on this. They had taken the unusual step of commenting on the newspaper report on O'Driscoll to say they did not believe he was involved in drugs.

As regards the Crinion murder, I said to Pat Kenny that if the drug-dealers of Mayfield knew anything about that, then they chose not to tell me, but I found no evidence of a drug war between northside and southside gangs. It was business as usual for the drug-dealers. I don't believe all this stuff about a drug war in Cork.

A few days later, *The Irish Times* praised my radio work with the Cork drug-dealers but doubted my judgment on there not being a drug war. But since then the weeks, months and now years have passed and there haven't been any more "hits". There was no drug war in Cork.

Over the following months, I was a bit scared to go back to Mayfield. I felt that I might be blamed for disrupting the drug trade there. Christmas week of 1995, I met some of the Mayfield druggies again. I was standing outside Cork Prison, making a programme for broadcast that week. Some young men who were in visiting a friend came out and reminded me that I interviewed them buying drugs in Mayfield. Their dealer, the cheerful one, was in prison. It was his own fault, they said, he didn't have to talk if he didn't want to. But the police shut down the Mayfield drug operation after I put that stuff on radio. The Super got fierce hassle off TDs and all. But things were okay again. For a while they used have to go into town to score but there's local fellahs dealing again. It's better to shop local if you can.

I was relieved that they didn't seem cross with me but it gave me no pleasure to have been involved in causing trouble to the cannabis-dealers of Cork. Do I think cannabis is harmless? No, I don't. Cannabis is at least as harmful as cigarettes. I think use of cannabis over a long period has bad effects on your lungs and probably your brain, too, just as alcoholic drink has all sorts of long-term health effects. But in terms of short-term effects, I think drink is much worse than cannabis.

Drink-related crime and drug-related crime, though often lumped together, are quite different. Drug-users steal to buy drugs. When they have their drugs they won't steal again until next time. Drinkers are different. It's after they are full of drink that they become dangerous.

A drunk may get violent, beat his wife or anybody else, drive a car, cause an accident, fall in a river, you name it.

Drink causes deaths, injury and suffering. Go into any district court on a Monday morning and you'll find that most of the violent crime over the weekend has been caused by drunks. Those young men in Mayfield weren't kidding when they said that they were always in trouble with the law until they discovered drugs. Now the worst they could expect would be an arrest for cannabis possession or for stealing. Even a stealing charge is less likely for them now than it would have been in their drinking days. A cannabis habit is cheaper to maintain than a drink habit.

(Heroin is different. It's expensive and addictive so junkies rob all the time. But, as with other drug-users, a heroin addict is harmless once his craving has been met. In Ireland, heroin is exclusively a Dublin drug.)

Those young people in Mayfield know that most of what they are told about drugs is rubbish. They think, rightly in my opinion, that their social betters haven't got a clue. There's no point telling young people to stay off drugs if you lecture them from a position of ignorance. And yet most advice that young people get about drugs is bad and ignorant advice.

In the Southern Health Board clinic in Mayfield, I picked up a leaflet on cannabis. All sorts of evil things are contrived about what cannabis does to you. Because the leaflet vastly overstates its case, any cannabis-smoker will dismiss it as nonsense and out of keeping with his own experience. Worse, the leaflet advises cannabis-smokers to look for help from the drug clinic at Trinity Court, Pearse Street in Dublin. Can you imagine if the young people of Cork took this advice seriously? Some Cork youngster turns up at Trinity Court, lines up with all the Dublin junkies looking for their methadone and then gets to tell the doctor that he's worried because he smoked a joint! I don't think the Southern Health Board is being sincere when it refers dope-smokers to Trinity Court in Dublin.

Another piece of nonsense that dope-smokers are told is that cannabis leads to heroin. Cork has been smoking cannabis for decades but there is no heroin in Cork. Working-class Dublin never had a cannabis habit but developed a horrific heroin habit about 1981.

The idea of cannabis as a gateway drug has now been acknowledged as a myth. In April of 1997, Pat Rabbitte, then chairman of the Government Task Force on Drugs, stated that studies in Dublin show that, contrary to popular opinion, people are most likely to start their drug habit with heroin and then move on to cannabis and other drugs, not the other way round. According to Rabbitte: "The model of gateways, and serial progression through a series of ever harder drugs, is grossly oversimplifying reality . . . heroin . . . is the predominant gateway."

Hallelujah! This is something that dope-smokers have always known but it's good to at last hear it from someone in a position of power. Rabbitte was looking at the drug problem with a view to saving lives rather than winning votes. That's unusual for a politician. It would be politically much safer for him to go on about dope-dealers being evil dealers in death and to suggest that any politician who says anything else is "soft on drugs". (This April 1997 statement from Rabbitte was, I think, the best thing to date from the Government Task Force on Drugs. The first report of the Task Force, in October 1996, claimed there was a heroin problem in Cork. I'll tell you more about the Cork heroin myth later.)

So now we know that cannabis doesn't lead to heroin. Rabbitte, in the same statement of April 1997, went on to say that this realisation confirmed the correctness of the

Government's approach, that is, giving primacy to tackling the heroin problem. All very fine, Minister. Tackle heroin first, I agree. But why don't you tell this to the police?

In 1995, the year I met those drug-dealers in Cork, there were 98 arrests for heroin possession or possession with intent to supply. In the same year there were over 3000 cannabis busts and more than half of these were in Cork, making the overall total for drug arrests in Cork higher than that for Dublin. Why? Dublin has a drug problem as bad as any in Europe. Cork's drug problem is nothing like as bad and yet police resources are aimed at cannabis in Cork rather than at the heroin problem in Dublin. What are the police at?

The high number of drug arrests in Cork in 1995, say the police, reflects arrests made at particular outdoor events. They mean the Féile, a big pop music event that took place in Cork that summer at which Kylie Minogue topped the bill. For the Féile, the police set up a courthouse in a tent and went on a feeding frenzy of arrests. One young friend of mine, an advertising salesman who works in Dublin, was smoking a joint, listening to the music, when the fellows next to him who were wearing jeans and bandanas produced their ID and arrested him. He was brought to the tent and convicted.

Why this zeal by the police and the judiciary to clamp down on cannabis when they don't show anything like that sense of urgency with other types of crime? The police are not stupid and they had to know that there would be no heroin at the Féile. A junkie has much more pressing things to do with £50 than go to see Kylie Minogue.

The police know, too, that dope-smokers don't cause trouble the way that drunks do. Cannabis, in my experience, makes people withdrawn and introspective, which is part of the reason I don't like it. Drink, my drug, makes people extroverted and relaxes inhibitions. Unfortunately, drink also impairs a person's judgment and some people can become reckless or violent when they drink. The police knew that the young dope-smokers at Féile, unlike drinkers, were not going to be causing trouble to anybody. And the police knew, too, that the Féile crowd, being young people, were unlikely to be driving cars, so they weren't going to be a danger to anybody on the roads.

But the police don't care about any of that. They only care about making the arrest figures look good and allowing the Minister for Justice to crow about being "tough on drugs". Fuck saving lives, there's promotions to be won.

Next time the police are so moved by the need to defeat crime that they take the step of setting up a court in a tent and inducing a judge to give up his Saturday afternoon golf, can I suggest that it be over something worthwhile? I'm sure there's plenty of other types of crime that we could all think of that the police could bring the same Féile-type zeal to bear on. And when the next drug bust figures come out, can we expect that the figures for heroin and cannabis busts will be reversed, that is, that there will be 98 cannabis seizures and over 3000 heroin seizures? That'll be the day. That's when I'll believe that the authorities are growing "tough on drugs".

Parents are given bad advice about drugs. I'm looking at a booklet from a Cork-based group. Parents are told that they should listen to their children and understand the seven reasons why young people take drugs. These reasons are, according to the Cork group: "to increase self-confidence on social occasions when shy or nervous; to help with difficulties of interpersonal relationships; as part of group activity; as a way of opting out of the adult world; to bolster themselves at a moment of uncertainty; as a means of escape when stress is overwhelming; as part of the curiosity and experimentation of youth".

Isn't there something missing here? Doesn't anyone consider that young people take drugs because they enjoy taking them? For all their talk of listening to what young people have to say, I don't think that much listening was done by the group who produced the above seven reasons for taking drugs.

We all know that young people are going to be exposed to drugs these days and that a lot of them will experiment. Most of them will survive this phase of their life, as I did, without coming to any harm. But, I think that underclass kids, such as those that I met in Mayfield, are more likely to go on taking drugs than are kids from better-off backgrounds.

When I was a student at UCC in the 1970s quite a lot of people in Cork smoked dope, although not nearly as many as do so today. Dope only ever made me feel sick and LSD scared me but, along with a few other teenage friends in Cobh, I enjoyed taking speed. We knew how to overdose on certain prescription drugs, usually slimming pills, in order to get high. We would all have a terrific night, probably not coming down and being able to sleep until about the middle of the next afternoon. I didn't take drugs because I was feeling socially inadequate, sexually confused, alienated from adult society or trying to cope with the emotional turmoil of something or other. I took drugs for the fun of it.

I reckon I took speed about a dozen times in all. I enjoyed it very much but I had other things in my life, too. I had a degree to study for and I was interested in writing and politics and music and travel and earning money. Since I moved to Dublin, aged twenty, I've never bothered with drugs again. I drink too much Guinness instead.

Underclass kids are different. Drugs are about the cheapest and best thrill they have available to them. You fill your life with drugs if you have nothing better to fill it with. And I think that might also explain why more men than women take drugs. I told you how it was all men buying dope that night in Mayfield. Underclass young men take to drugs because there is so little else in life for them.

The women have babies and get paid for being mothers which means they have a job and responsibility. A young mother's boyfriend has no job or responsibility. It's only if the man can get a reliable job that pays more than his and his girlfriend's welfare combined that he can suggest to his child's mother that he and she should marry or at least set up home together. Reliable, decently-paid jobs barely exist for underclass men. If, on welfare, a father tries to move in with his partner and child and be a proper dad, he will jeopardise his partner's lone parent's pay. The social welfare system makes young fathers worse than useless to their girlfriends and children.

In a welfare ghetto, drug-dealing is the most obvious form of local entrepreneurial activity that a young person is likely to see. Young, underclass men will become drug-dealers because they see the money to be made, even by people such as themselves for whom most other paths of advancement are closed off. It beats the hell out of yet another FÁS course.

So I get no joy from knowing that I caused difficulties

for the drug-dealers of Cork. I think it's sad that those young men I met in Mayfield have nothing better in their lives than cannabis but I don't want to take that away from them, too.

Dungarvan and the Heterosexual Aids Myth

There was no outbreak of Aids in Dungarvan. The Sunday night in September 1995 before the Dungarvan story broke, I sent an article to the *Cork Examiner* saying that heterosexual Aids in Ireland was a myth. The next morning the *Examiner* headline read that five men in Dungarvan had Aids. The source of the story was a local priest, Michael Kennedy, who gave a sermon at Mass the day before. He said the men were deliberately infected by an HIV-positive woman who was seeking revenge on the male sex in general for having herself been infected.

I saw the *Examiner* headline early on Monday morning. Immediately I phoned with a postscript to my article to say that I didn't believe the Dungarvan story and that if there was an outbreak of Aids in that town, the only explanation was that the source of the infection was an HIV-positive man. The *Examiner* published my article the next day, along with my postscript.

A few days later, I was in Dungarvan and I'll tell you about that experience shortly. But since long before Dungarvan, I have argued publicly that heterosexual Aids in Ireland is a myth.

I first touched on this in my last book *Queueing for a Living*. I wrote about Frances Flynn, who was HIV-positive, and Mick who was her lover. Frances was in her mid-thirties when she met Mick who was about ten years older. Mick had worked in Britain and the USA. He never had anything to do with drugs and, when he first met Frances, he knew very little about Aids. Frances was a junkie on methadone maintenance and Mick did his best to help her to stay away from heroin.

I remember once when Frances was very ill, I gave her a lift one day to Pearse Street and Mick and I carried her from my car into the clinic. Mick told me later, it's not because I feel sorry for her that I stay with her. It's because I love her. But this fucking Aids yoke, I must surely have the fucking thing by now, Pat, but at least I enjoyed meself getting it. (Working-class Dubliners rarely use the name Paddy. They call me either *Paah*trick or Pa'h.)

Don't think that Mick, I said. There's been a lot of misinformation put about on how Aids is spread. I told him that the chance of his having caught the virus through sex with Frances was very small. Frances died in January of 1993. I don't know if Mick was ever tested for the virus but he remains alive and well today.

We have all been lied to about heterosexual Aids. I don't believe the figures provided by the Department of Health. For the last ten years or more, the Department has claimed that 15% of HIV sufferers in Ireland caught the virus through heterosexual sex. Every six months or so, the new Aids figures come out and the 15% figure gets repeated by politicians and journalists alike. Successive health ministers continue to use the 15% figure, even though I have many times pointed out to the Department of Health that this figure is based on very poor evidence.

If you look at the Department's press releases on the latest Aids figures, you will see that they include a footnote which I think is important but which always gets overlooked in the press coverage. It reads like this: "The above figures which are produced by the Virus Reference Laboratory relate to categories of persons as identified by the patients themselves or by their clinicians." So the evidence we have for heterosexual Aids in Ireland is that 15% of infected persons claim they caught the virus through heterosexual sex.

It doesn't seem to occur to the Department of Health that people might lie about how they caught the virus. A secret homosexual or bisexual might lie to his friends or family about what he was doing.

Or let's take someone who is a secret drug user. More than once I have heard distraught Dublin mothers claim that their little girl never took anything more than an aspirin and that she caught the disease from that bad man who was her boyfriend. I remember one case in the 1980s. I'll call her Mary. Mary's mother was on television, radio and the newspapers about heterosexual Aids. I didn't know Mary personally but I knew a lot of her family and one sister in particular whom I had interviewed outside drug clinics in London as well as in Dublin. Of eleven children in Mary's family, nine became drug addicts and two, including Mary, have since died from the virus. One afternoon I was in Mary's house in Crumlin and Mary's mother was doing her usual thing, cursing her son-in-law for infecting her daughter. My friend, Mary's older sister, eventually lost her patience. Ma, please stop winding up Pat (that's me) and winding yourself up along with everybody else. Mary's been turning on for as long as I have.

Let's try to get a closer look at the people who make up the 15% of alleged heterosexual Aids victims. I have tried for years, without success, to get the Department of Health to give further details on this 15% figure. Specifically, how many of these heterosexuals are men and how many are women?

This information is not available. Patient confidentiality, says the Department.

I don't accept that answer. We are told exactly how many drug users who are HIV-positive are men and how many are women, but the Department keeps its information on heterosexuals secret. Why so? Are the junkies not entitled to the same privacy as these supposed heterosexuals?

Among HIV-positive junkies, according to Department figures, men outnumber women approximately three-to-one. This information is of interest and demands explanation but it tells us nothing that we didn't know already about how the virus is spread. Stick an infected needle in your arm and you can catch Aids.

But a sex breakdown on the 15% supposed heterosexuals would be useful. If we knew how many were men and how many were women, it would tell us a lot about how the virus is spread. Which is the greater risk, man-to-woman or woman-to-man? And of the women who have been infected, it would be important to know what particular sexual practices they were involved in.

If there is a case of a woman having caught the virus through sex, I would like to know what she was doing and with whom. Supposing she was with a man who was a secret bisexual who preferred sex in a way that allowed him to imagine that he was with his boyfriend. It makes sense to me that receptive, anal sex is just as dangerous for a woman as it is for a man. If a woman should catch the virus in this way, I don't think that can be called a case of heterosexual transmission as is commonly understood.

Now, please bear with me while I do a bit of mathematics in order to show that the Department's heterosexual Aids claim is nonsense. Even though the Department of Health won't give any more detail on its figures for heterosexual

Aids, it does give a breakdown by sex for its overall Aids figures. Let's take the figures issued for the total of Aids cases and Aids deaths up to the end of 1996. Of these, 728 are men and 153 are women, making a total of 881.

From these male and female totals, I'm going to deduct those groups for which there is no way of guessing what sex they might be. There are a total of 33 who are listed as "children born to drug addicts", "other children" and "undetermined". I'll also deduct the 15 who are listed as "homo/bisexual/IVDU". I thought first about assuming that this group were all men but, as I know a lot of lesbians who are intravenous drug users (IVDU), I'll add them to the other 33 whose sex we don't know. So let's deduct the total of 48 on a basis of 24 fewer men and 24 fewer women leaving a new male total of 704 and a female total of 129.

From the male total of 704 I'm going to deduct the 55 haemophiliacs who are, of course, all men, and the 296 homosexuals and bisexuals who I am assuming are all men. (Again, the Department won't give a sex breakdown on its homo/bisexual figures. That's a pity because if, as I believe, there are no women in this group, that would indicate that lesbian-type activities don't spread the virus. That would be useful information for all of us in trying to work out what constitutes safe sex.) Our new male total, which is now made up of just drug addicts and heterosexuals, is 353. Our female total for same is still 129.

Now let's subtract the 386 junkies. There's not a sex breakdown given for this number but we do know from Department figures for HIV-positive junkies, as distinct from actual Aids cases, that men in this category outnumber women by approximately three to one. So let's carry that proportion into the 386 Aids cases and say that 289 are men and 97 are women. Subtract these from our male and female totals and that leaves us with a final figure for the heterosexuals of 64 men and 32 women. So the men outnumber the women by two to one.

That's an extraordinary figure. Irish women's vaginas must be the most dangerous in the world. Nowhere else but in Ireland do women have the power to infect men to twice the degree that men have to infect women. Of course, it can be said that I've just done a lot of rough reckoning to arrive at those figures, but the gross imbalance of men over women is too great to be a product of simply too many assumptions on my part.

A male majority would be inexplicable in terms of heterosexual transmission. Such evidence that there is suggests that, in so far as there is any risk of heterosexual transmission, women are more at risk than men. Body fluids during sexual intercourse go overwhelmingly one way. No wonder the Department of Health won't issue the sex breakdown that I ask for on heterosexuals. The result would show up the heterosexual Aids claim for the cod that it is.

Next, let's try to find one of these 15% supposed heterosexual victims. What I'm looking for here is what the social scientists scorn as "anecdotal" evidence. To me, the absence, after all these years, of anecdotal evidence for heterosexual Aids raises serious doubts about the 15% claim. If there were heterosexuals catching Aids, some of them would be talking about it.

Let us say a young man goes to a disco one night. He meets a gorgeous young woman and after a night of passion he discovers, some weeks later, that he has caught Aids. If this was really happening, the way the Aids awareness industry (henceforth the AAI) is saying that it is, then at least some young men such as this one would be talking publicly about the experience. There is no taboo against casual heterosexual sex. Rather, young men are likely to be boastful about their conquests. Homosexual sex is still taboo but I have heard plenty of homosexuals with Aids speaking as interviewees to Gay Byrne, Gerry Ryan and so on. The AAI would love to hear an interview from a male victim of heterosexual transmission. The condom industry would pay a fortune for such an interview. But no such interview has been heard. They seem to be a very silent lot, this 15%.

Next, think about your own friends and acquaintances. Do you know anybody, man or woman, who has caught the virus heterosexually? Speaking for myself, I have, through my work, met countless junkies who have caught Aids. Outside of work, I can think of two homosexual men, both from Cobh, Co Cork, whom I knew personally and who died from the Aids virus. But I have never known, or heard of, any person who caught Aids through heterosexual sex.

Next think about famous people with Aids. We can all think of actors, pop stars and so on who have died of the virus. Freddie Mercury, Tom McGinty (The Diceman), Rudolf Nureyev, Liberace, Brad Davis, Kenny Everett, Denholm Eliot, Anthony Perkins, Rock Hudson, Russell Harty. The list goes on. But there are no women on that list and all the men were either homosexual or bisexual. Where are the heterosexuals? Surely if the figure was 15% in Ireland and in the developed world generally we would have heard of somebody famous getting it by now?

But the Department sticks to its 15% figure and the AAI continues to go on with the same old scare-mongering. Go into your local health board and pick up a leaflet on Aids. Rectal and vaginal sex are treated as if both were equally risky activities.

I remember the Aids "education" campaign in Britain in the early 1990s. Huge billboards showed a collection of about thirty people of both sexes, all ages, all ethnic groups and all walks of life. Anybody can get Aids, said the slogan. This poster campaign was a triumph for the AAI in promoting its own importance but a disaster in terms of promoting understanding of, and stopping the spread of, the Aids virus.

Every few months you see yet another social worker or AAI activist warning about the need for more money for their own project or else we'll all catch the virus. In 1996 the Eastern Health Board got money from the EU's anti-Aids fund to publish a silly study on prostitution in Dublin. The report was full of useless information. We were told, solemnly, that 94% of prostitutes do it for the money. I'm still dying to know what the other 6% do it for but the study didn't say.

A great deal of detail was gone into about what particular activities prostitutes get up to with their clients. Bar charts, pie charts, graphs and so on were produced to show how many whores do or don't do oral/anal/vaginal/manual/verbal/armpit/bondage/discipline/stick things up his arse or whatever. I enjoyed the two women who consistently answered "don't know" to all questions. My theory is that they were in the Health Board office to apply for a medical card and that they were given the wrong form to fill out.

The report told us nothing about the spread of Aids. None of the 84 prostitutes who responded to the Eastern Health Board study were HIV-positive. That makes for an absurd sample group. There are plenty of HIV-positive women among Dublin's prostitutes but these are all junkies who got it from the needle. If any female prostitutes should be studied about Aids and its possible spread through sex then it is the HIV-positive women on Benburb Street. But the AAI isn't interested in an honest study of these women. My belief is that if a proper study was carried out it would show that none of the Benburb Street women's clients have ever caught Aids.

But the AAI doesn't care about getting at the truth. It only cares about spreading a climate of fear and therefore boosting its own importance and chances of getting more public money for its projects.

In 1997 the Mid-Western Health Board emulated the Eastern Health Board and looked for money to combat Aids among prostitutes in Limerick. The Limerick study, if it goes ahead, will fail to turn up any HIV-positive female prostitutes because there are none. But that won't bother the social workers and the AAI. Expect the MWHB, if it ever produces its Aids report, to come up with a vague, generalised scare about Aids and the need for more "education", but you can be sure that the report will be short on specifics about Aids in Limerick.

It's not just in Ireland that the AAI seeks to confuse people. Early in 1997, random sampling of out-patients in Britain showed that Aids is at its worst in the poorest, inner-city areas. The Terence Higgins Trust was brought on to *Sky News* to interpret the data. It's not clear how people are getting it, said the Trust, but there is evidence that homosexuals are getting careless again and what we really need now is for everybody to be careful and, you guessed it, more money for Aids awareness. Nobody mentioned intravenous drug use.

I don't believe that working-class Englishmen are more prone to homosexual activity than are their middle-class fellow-countrymen. But I know that heroin addiction is at its worst in the inner cities so there's no mystery about why Aids is at its worst in the same areas. But the AAI thrives on mystery rather than on public understanding about the real causes of Aids.

I think historians will look back on the AAI era as having been the era of the greatest disinformation campaign ever carried out against the people of the free world. The AAI spreads fear, misunderstanding and ignorance. Sleep with one person and you are sleeping with several hundreds of that person's previous partners and their previous partners and so on. Remember all that? They would terrify you. You think back over your life and worry about every sexual experience you ever had. When you were fourteen behind the school shed and you showed your willy to your girlfriend, did you get Aids? They'd have you scared of your own right hand.

I have looked beyond Ireland to try to find evidence of heterosexual Aids. I have read the newspaper scare-stories for years and I have trawled the Internet. Even the minuscule evidence that I've found for heterosexual Aids is, in my opinion, suspect. Some studies claim there is a one-in-five-hundred chance of a woman catching Aids through heterosexual intercourse with an infected person and about a one-in-a-thousand risk for a man. I think those figures exaggerate the risk.

The people included in studies on heterosexual Aids in Britain, the USA and elsewhere, are not healthy heterosexuals. They are unhealthy people, such as the sexual partners of drug addicts. Often they have other sexually transmissible diseases that make the body more vulnerable to infection with the Aids virus. Let us take a woman who has sex 500 times with her junkie partner and gets infected. Such a woman was unlikely to be a healthy heterosexual in the first place. It isn't tenable, in my view, to calculate a level of risk for a healthy heterosexual woman or man on the basis of infection rates observed among the sort of poor, sick heterosexuals who tend to have the virus.

Do you remember those AAI adverts on the telly about

heterosexual Aids? In one that I particularly disliked, a fellow is in a pub and he meets a very sexy, healthy-looking young woman. He gets off with her and some weeks later he discovers he has the virus. The camera shows her again. She's beautiful with delicious, kissable lips. A doom-laden, middle-class voice of authority tells us, you can't tell an Aids-carrier to look at one.

I hated that advert. For one, it was typical AAI disinformation. It's true that you can't tell an Aids-carrier to look at one but you can make a reasonable guess, by the look of them, about the sort of people you should avoid sex with. Whores, junkies and the sexual partners of either of these categories don't look healthy. If you lead a healthy lifestyle and have a bit of common sense you would keep away from having sex with those types of heterosexuals. And yet the AAI is trying to tell me that the beautiful, healthy-looking young woman in the advert is capable of killing me.

I hated that advert even more because of its attitude towards sex. The AAI try to spoil the fun and excitement of getting off with somebody by threatening you with the remote chance of getting Aids. No wonder the AAI has attracted totalitarians of both Right and Left to its ranks. People might be having fun. Let's spoil it for them. People are exercising free choice. Let's try to control their behaviour.

I mean, fuck it all, even if there is a remote chance of getting Aids from a healthy-looking heterosexual like that gorgeous woman in the advert, surely we take bigger risks all the time in just getting on with our lives? I think I would stand a bigger risk of being killed in a car crash on my way to that gorgeous lady's house. But will I give up my evening of enjoyment because of the risk of a road accident? Who wants to live that way?

In Africa, Aids does spread through heterosexual sex. Aids in Africa has been massively more destructive than it has been in Europe or North America. A lot of the spread in Africa has probably been due to poor hygiene and the repeated use of needles in hard-pressed health clinics. This was how the Ebola virus was spread in parts of central Africa some years ago. But Aids in Africa is also spread through heterosexual sex, especially, I am told by experts, if some other form of venereal disease, such as syphilis, is also present. The lesions caused by venereal disease make a person's skin vulnerable to penetration by the Aids virus.

Venereal disease is widespread in Africa because where you have poverty, you have prostitution. I remember in Addis Ababa and in rural Ethiopia generally, every bar or cafe seemed to have a room out the back for sex with the female staff. Poor young women in Africa routinely turn to prostitution to augment their income, as was the case with poor young women in Europe in centuries past. The original Molly Malone in Dublin, I am told by historians, sold more than just cockles and mussels.

So Aids in Africa is fueled by poverty, the prostitution that goes with poverty and also by poor medical care. These conditions don't exist in Europe and North America and yet the AAI – and I have seen this – uses Third World statistics to spread fear and confusion about the spread of Aids in the First World. The AAI would serve us better if it would tell the truth, target its message where it is needed at the junkies and male homosexuals and stop crying wolf about heterosexual Aids.

Which brings me back to Dungarvan. After years of generating a climate of fear, something like the Dungarvan scare was bound to happen. It was a priest who spread the story but it was the social workers and the AAI who had made people ready to believe it.

Dungarvan, Co Waterford;
September 1995

If there was really an Aids outbreak in Dungarvan it had to be caused by a man. The same man had buggered and infected all five men or else, having buggered one, they had all gone on to bugger and infect each other. No other explanation. But who was the man?

I came up with a theory on this that I knew from the start was extravagant, and that I can't repeat now, but at least it was more within the realms of possibility than was the Angel of Death theory. I approached the *Today at Five* programme and told them I thought there was no Angel of Death and that if there was Aids being spread, I thought I knew who the bugger was. *Today at Five* sent me to Dungarvan.

I was driving to Dungarvan a few days after the story first broke. The story was being covered again on the radio as I drove south. I listened carefully, just as I had been watching the newspapers closely as the story unfolded. Good journalists reported the claims made by Kennedy as claims. Bad journalists reported these claims as "revelations". Kennedy rewarded the bad journalists with further interviews. The result was a series of rubbish stories.

A woman claimed that she was infected by one of the Dungarvan men who was infected by the Angel of Death. She got headlines in the newspaper she spoke to. The same newspaper, over the next few days, continued to run the "exclusives" it was getting from this woman. She even got onto *Sky News*. When it was realised that she was not a person to be believed, but rather a person to be pitied, her story was quietly dropped. But her story should have been seen through straight away. It was the myth of heterosexual Aids that caused the media and the public alike to believe her in the first place.

I arrived in Dungarvan. It was full of media people, as was to be expected. Journalists told me that Kennedy had gone to ground. That suited me fine. Kennedy had already been asked all the pertinent questions so there was nothing more for me to ask him. I had other things on my mind.

I needed to speak to young men. The first group I approached were at the quayside. They were in their late teens, smoking cigarettes after school. It's easy to get young men to talk. They are boastful. They all knew who the Angel of Death was but they weren't prepared to tell me. She was English, they said. She was apart from her husband and sometimes goes to pubs in town. She wears a short skirt and make-up. Sure, what's the fuss about, they asked? This kind of thing happens in Dublin all the time and there's nothing said about it. It's only because it's here in Dungarven that there's all this fuss.

I told them that nothing like this had ever happened in Dublin. There are no men catching Aids from women. If the Dungarvan story turns out to be true, then it's a very important story that deserves every bit of the fuss that's being made of it.

I didn't argue with them too much. You need to make people feel that they are talking sense if you want to get them to talk to you. But I knew they were talking rubbish. A woman with late Aids is in no condition to go around seducing anyone. The images of my two late friends, Rose Waldron and Frances Flynn, kept going through my mind.

I remember going to see Rose at her home in Bluebell just a few weeks before she died. She looked about twice her forty years of age as she sat propped up in her bed. She was small and shriveled. Her cheeks were collapsed and her skin was tight against her skull. Her nightdress gave the impression of being on a coat-hanger, rather than on a woman's body. Most of her hair had fallen out. Her skin was red and tormented with ulcers. Her lips, tongue and mouth were cracked and blistered with some kind of fungal infection. Her eyes were bloodshot and staring out of deep, cadaverous sockets in her skull. She was no longer sure what was real or imagined, she told me. She heard voices she couldn't explain and kept seeing her late mother standing at the foot of her bed. Her fingers were bloody stumps where some of her nails had been amputated because of infection. Her voice was rasping from the destruction of her lungs. And I remember her repeated, frustrated attempts to get a cigarette out of a packet, not realising that the packet was empty.

That was Rose. Once I read a letter in *The Irish Times* from someone in the AAI saying that we shouldn't refer to Aids victims or sufferers as Aids victims or sufferers. Something to do with not stigmatising them. The AAI is full of stupid ideas. Rose suffered.

I remember Frances Flynn. She could barely walk in the end. She would often wet or soil her pants as the Aids virus wiped out more and more of her body's self-control. It was something new every day, Frances said. Her lungs one day, her bowels or bladder the next, then her sight, her balance, her muscles. If God wants me so much I wish he'd fucking take me, said Frances, and stop doing all this to me. As Frances lay asleep some of the contents of her belly used to disgorge through her mouth and go down her chest in long brown trickles. Frances looked dead long before she died.

I'm feeling angry now again as I write this. Same as I felt angry that day in Dungarvan. The suffering of Rose and Frances was the reality of late Aids. Rose or Frances would not have been able to pull horny young men at discos. And yet Father Michael Kennedy had the young people of Dungarvan believing that a woman in late Aids was going around the pubs and clubs seducing fellows. She seduced eighty men in a few months, said Kennedy. I knew Kennedy was talking nonsense but the people were believing him.

At the town square of Dungarvan, Cork Aids Alliance had set up a stall. They were handing out leaflets, peddling the same old rubbish about heterosexual Aids. Rectal and vaginal sex were presented as equally risky activities. Well done, folks. You certainly have got your message across to the public. Aids is not a gay plague, you say. We are all equally at risk, you say. Now, look around you in Dungarvan and see what you've done. People believe you. If you believe the AAI nonsense about heterosexual Aids then the Angel of Death story seems entirely credible.

I wandered the town to see who else might talk to me. A group of young people were sitting at the central square. The women wouldn't talk but the men were full of it. That woman was going to be run out of town, they said, after what she did to those lads. They knew very well who she was. She's from Dungarvan. She's an unmarried mother with two children. She goes out to pubs when she should be looking after her kids.

A shopkeeper told me the Angel of Death had left town. He knew who she was. She always wore a short skirt and took advantage of local lads. She was home from America over the summer but she won't be welcome back any more. Another shopkeeper recognised who I was, probably because

I was wearing my hat. Don't believe a word of it, Paddy, he said. This whole Aids story is rubbish.

It was clear to me now. The Angel of Death was any woman in Dungarvan who didn't fit a pattern of virginity during youth followed by meek self-sacrifice for marriage and children. Any woman of an independent spirit was a candidate for being the Angel of Death. It was reaching 5 p.m. Time to phone RTE. A short while later I was on the air, talking to Myles Dungan.

There is no Angel of Death. I have spent the day talking to people in Dungarvan and, of those who believe the story, they all have different versions of who this woman is.

Myles Dungan asked me if Father Kennedy had ever checked to see if the young men who were supposed to have Aids had ever had a drug habit. A good question and I didn't know the answer. But I answered that it was extremely unlikely that there could be an Aids outbreak in Dungarvan through intravenous drug use. There is no heroin in Ireland anywhere outside of Dublin. It was just possible that one or two men might have developed a heroin habit in Dublin or maybe London and then returned to Dungarvan after giving up drugs. But a town the size of Dungarvan couldn't sustain a community of five or more addicts. (I'll explain more about this later when I tell you about another story that never was, the heroin problem in Cork.)

I tried to keep the irritation out of my voice as I dealt with the idea of a seductress going around the discos. Kennedy had no understanding of what Aids is really like, I said.

I might have added, but didn't, that Kennedy had the oddest notion of the way that Aids affects a victim. The only immediate sign of infection is a slight rash and a fever that passes after a day or so. The victim probably doesn't know that he or she has been infected. Intravenous drug-users might become ill after a couple of years, while people who have been sexually infected take longer to go full-blown. (The difference is that Aids is more virulent when delivered in blood than it is when delivered through sex. I owe my information here to Frank Ryan's 1996 book *Virus X*, about emerging viruses in the modern world.) And yet Kennedy was telling us that five young men had developed symptoms just weeks after having a ride, confided in each other, concluded they had Aids and then had come to him for help. Did Kennedy think they were all examining their mickeys and finding evidence of Aids infection? The fellow hadn't a clue.

The whole story is bunk, I told Myles Dungan. There is no Angel of Death and there is no Aids outbreak in Dungarvan.

Heroin in Cork (in memory of Niamh)
Radio Centre, RTE;
October 1996

Niamh was on my mind for two reasons. One, it was ten years since her death. She died in London. She lived there along with a number of other junkies from Cork city and County. I was back in Dublin now but just a few days before in London I had stood outside what was Niamh's house in Kilburn and said whatever kind of prayer it is that a living atheist can say to a dead one. You told me, Niamh, that you could handle heroin, that it's only careless junkies who overdose. Don't worry, Paddy. You could handle London, you said. You would be fine. You fool, Niamh. I miss you.

Niamh was on my mind for a second reason, too. When I got back to Dublin at the weekend I read in the newspapers about the launch of the First Report of the Government Task Force on Drugs. This first report was on the heroin problem,

51

which the Task Force said it regarded as the most pressing of all drug problems, a view that I certainly agree with. Heroin kills, cannabis doesn't. But there was something else in that report that shocked me and that I found hard to accept. Heroin was no longer confined to Dublin. According to the Task Force, heroin was also in Cork.

How could that be? I thought I knew Cork and its drug scene well. So far as I knew, the heroin problem in Cork ended about 1980 when the small number of junkies in that city, about ten in all including Niamh, moved to London where they since died.

In Cork, those junkies used to hang around in a city centre pub. Even then, in the 1970s, heroin was a working-class thing, as it would be in Dublin in the following decade on a vastly greater scale. Cork's junkies, with the exception of Niamh, spoke with strong working-class accents. Niamh, I remember, adopted the working-class accent of her fellow-junkies. That's a pattern I see in Dublin to this day on the rare occasions when a middle-class kid becomes a heroin-addict. I know one Dublin father in a good job who tells me that when his daughter became a junkie her accent changed along with every other aspect of her life. She gave up her old friends and took on the accent of her fellow-junkies of Dolphin's Barn.

Cannabis, in Cork in the 1970s, was a middle-class thing. The dope-smokers I knew at UCC and Crawford School of Art went on to get good jobs and, for all I know, are still smoking dope today. Likewise in Dublin, cannabis in the 1970s was mainly a habit of the young middle-class. The places to get dope in Dublin were Trinity College or else the trendy pubs and cafes around the Dandelion Market at St Stephen's Green.

Then, about 1981, the drug scene in Ireland changed profoundly. After the fall of the Shah of Iran, heroin hit the world and Dublin was one of the places it hit hardest. Working-class Dublin took to heroin with an ardour that, to me, still beggars belief and defies adequate explanation. There was a lot of talk in the 1970s and since about cannabis being a "gateway" drug to worse forms of abuse but working-class Dublin needed no gateway. They never smoked dope. They went straight for heroin.

So now, in 1996, we were being told by the Government Task Force on Drugs that heroin was no longer confined to Dublin. I had always dreaded the thought that this day would come, that the heroin disaster of Dublin would become a national disaster, affecting every town and village in the country. Up until now, I had always found a sense of relief when dealing with working-class kids in Cork or Belfast. They smoke a lot of dope and pop a lot of pills but they don't do heroin. The drug problem in Cork and Belfast is as nothing compared to that of Dublin.

And why had heroin remained confined to Dublin? I'm not entirely sure, but I think it has a lot to do with its price. A heroin habit is costly. Every morning in Dublin, a small army of junkies wake up and all of them need to raise £50 to £100 to get their turn-on and keep their desperation for drugs at bay for another few hours. They rob from shops, cars and houses and they sell what they steal. To sustain a population of junkies, a city needs to be above a certain size. An average Irish town isn't big enough to allow junkies to shoplift and burgle and dispose of their takings on a daily basis. In an average town, any junkie would quickly become well known to everyone and would be forced to go to Dublin or England to keep up his drug habit, just as Niamh and her pals were forced to leave Cork around 1980 when they had become too well known to the police. So heroin never took root in Ireland outside of Dublin. But now I was being told there was heroin in Cork.

Could it be true? Was it possible that a task force of experts could be mistaken? Or was I the one who had been mistaken to date, being too blind, in all the times I had worked on drugs in Cork, to see that a heroin problem was developing? I was sorry I had missed the press conference on Friday. I knew I was going to have a lot of questions to ask the Government on Monday morning. The press reports indicated that the heroin problem on Cork's northside was as bad as it was in ten named areas of Dublin. So how many addicts in Cork? Are they registered addicts and if so are they receiving methadone maintenance? When was the Cork heroin problem first detected? How many heroin seizures have there been?

Monday came and I phoned the office of Pat Rabbitte, Minister of State at the Taoiseach's Department. Rabbitte was chairman of the Task Force on Drugs. The press officer arranged to send me a copy of the report but the person who could answer my questions wasn't available today. I left a message on his voice mail.

When I got the report it was all there as reported in the papers. Heroin in Dublin and Cork. Ten areas of Dublin and one on the northside of Cork city. These eleven areas of heroin abuse would be given top priority by the Government with waiting lists for treatment eliminated in the Eastern Health Board area within five years.

That read strangely. Why only in the Eastern Health Board area? Are Cork junkies not worthy of the same attention as Dublin ones?

I looked to find the section of the report dealing with Cork. There was none. There were detailed maps of Dublin and Dun Laoghaire showing the extent of heroin abuse in various suburbs. Figures were given for people registered for methadone maintenance. But what of Cork? All there was, repeated throughout, was an assertion about a "cluster" of heroin addicts in Cork. No maps or figures. Was this cluster made up of thousands of addicts as in Dublin? Hundreds, perhaps? Or maybe ten? No clue was given. There was no evidence to support the assertion about heroin in Cork. My suspicion about the Government Task Force report on heroin in Cork was turning to certainty. It was complete shite.

I phoned a Government press officer whose brief I thought was relevant. She was irritated at me because of things I had said before about the government being wrong on heterosexual Aids. You always think you know best, don't you, Paddy? There's heroin in every town in Ireland but Paddy O'Gorman says there's no heroin in Cork. What makes you think you know better than a task force of experts?

I phoned the Southern Health Board. Who told the Task Force that there was a heroin problem in Cork? The Board would only give me a line that they were studying the drug problem generally and that there would be a report in the future. How many registered heroin addicts are there in Cork? No comment. Is there anybody on methadone maintenance in the Southern Health Board area? No comment. (The Southern Health Board finally answered those last two questions the following May. The answers are none and no.)

I phoned the Garda Press Office. Any figures for heroin seizures in Cork? The most recent figures available were for 1995. In that year there was a total of 1730 drug offences in the east Cork division, which includes Cork city. Of these, the figure for heroin offences was 2. (I remembered one of those offences when it was reported in the *Cork Examiner*. He was a Dubliner arrested for shoplifting and found to have heroin on him. Dublin junkies often travel to shoplift once they have become too well known to Dublin store detectives.) The figure for West Cork was 0. The figure for 1994 heroin offences in Cork was 0. A few hours later the Garda Press Office phoned me back to tell me that they had no reports of any increase, dramatic or otherwise, of the incidence of heroin in Cork.

I felt angry but the anger was a good feeling. Instead of dealing with a heroin tragedy all we had was a report inspired by politicians. It seemed to me that they didn't want all the money to be seen to be going to Dublin so they had invented a heroin problem in Cork. Instead of addressing the heroin problem they were addressing electoral considerations. I don't exactly know the meaning of the word but, for some reason, the term "gombeen" kept coming into my mind.

I was on a high. I'll teach those fuckers to mess with people's lives. It was October 15, the tenth anniversary of Niamh's death. I wanted to remember Niamh in some way and now I had found a way to do it. I was working on *Today at Five* that afternoon and now I had a story. I went to the word processor and typed up my thoughts. The heroin problem that never was. I wrote from my own knowledge of drugs in Cork, past and present. I wrote up the Garda figures. I rubbished the claims of the Government Task Force. And I wrote about Niamh.

I printed off my two pages of writings and put it on the desk of the *Today at Five* producer Ronan O'Donoghue. Ronan came back to me a few minutes later. Right, he said. Get yourself down to studio.

It was about 5.30 p.m. when I went in to be interviewed by Myles Dungan. I was nervous, about to say publicly that a panel of supposed experts had got their facts all wrong. I said a prayer on my way in. This one's for you, Niamh.

I was deliberately provocative. I had been two days asking what figures were available on the alleged heroin problem in Cork and Rabbitte's office was clearly not going to answer. They were hoping I would just go away. Perhaps I could goad them into a reply. (To date, I have failed.)

I went through the Garda figures with Myles. Heroin comes to the attention of the police much more quickly than say, cocaine or LSD, as was explained in a copy of *Garda Review* some years ago in an article by its then editor, Stephen Rae. Heroin is expensive and used by poor people, whereas cocaine is not so expensive and is used by people with money. So heroin addicts rob and quickly come to the attention of the police whereas a cocaine-user could be putting white stuff up his nose for years without the police knowing it. If there was heroin in Cork the police would know about it and yet the Government was claiming to know about a heroin problem that had escaped the notice of the police.

I talked about Aids. If you have a heroin problem you will also have an Aids problem. A few years ago, there was a report from Cork showing that the Aids virus in that city was a sexually transmitted disease rather than a disease of drug users. This was puzzled over at the time. Why was Cork so different to Dublin? In fact there was no mystery about this difference. It's because the type of drugs used in Cork are not intravenously-taken drugs. No heroin, no needles, no Aids. You can't get Aids from smoking dope or popping pills.

Taking a prompt from me, Myles asked me if there was ever heroin in Cork. Yes, Myles, there once was. I told him about the very small number of addicts in Cork twenty years ago. They had all gone to London where, to my knowledge, a number of them, perhaps all of them, had since died. One of them, Myles, was a dear friend of mine, Niamh, who died ten years ago today.

I was glad to tell the world again that Niamh was my friend. I was proud of her as a friend even though I hated her heroin habit. Now I had remembered her on her anniversary. I did it for you, Niamh.

Chapter Three

Manchester
Department of Social Security, Cheetham Hill;
October 1994

Cheetham, I'm told, was once an Irish and Jewish district. It's black and Asian now. There are open-air markets here. The stalls are run by men with turbans and black beards. I was standing at the DSS entrance, around the side of a shopping centre and looking into an old, overgrown graveyard. I was in the DSS foyer. There's a dirty smell in there. The carpet is filthy and covered with cigarette burns but at least I was in from the cold.

So far on my first day here, the only Irish I had met were travellers. There was a big family of them waiting in the DSS. Once I stopped one of the children from running out on the road and, for my trouble, I was abused by one of the young women, the child's aunt or older sister, I guess. Kathleen, Kathleen, he won't layve the child alone. After that I ignored them. They were an unfriendly lot.

Two middle-aged men came out. They had cans of beer and rural Irish accents. They seemed suspicious of me, as if they didn't believe me that I was from RTE. No, they wouldn't talk.

I'm sure they would have been interesting. Probably they came here decades ago. They worked the buildings and now, too old for that, they were unemployed. They bought cans of drink because your money stretches further that way than it would if you were in the pub. I guess they were single, like so many Irish builders of their generation. It's a lonely life for them here in Manchester, but it would probably be even lonelier back in Ireland.

I was put in mind of other men who came here in the 1950s and 1960s and who did better. I remember the first time I was here in Cheetham, back in 1987, I interviewed a group of older Irishmen in a pub. They had all done well and had children and grandchildren here. I remember their anti-Dublin bias which I found interesting. You should never employ a Dublin man. A Dublin man came to me once looking for the shtart and he had a pair of hush-puppies on him. I said go way, boy, and get yourself a pair of boots. Don't employ a Dublin man because he's no good for doing any work.

This anti-Dublin prejudice is something I have found in the London and New York building industries many times. I have interviewed Dubliners in the early mornings at Cricklewood Broadway in London and, in New York, at Bainbridge Avenue in the Bronx and Daytona Avenue in Yonkers, all waiting for their "subbies" to pick them up for the day. They only want big Mayo men, one Dub told me. Culchies only want to employ other culchies like themselves. Like most prejudices, this anti-Dublin one has, I think, some basis in truth. Rural men tend to be physically bigger than working-class Dublin men. That's still the case today and was much more the case in decades and centuries past.

The great days of the Irish building industry here in Manchester are now gone. The young Irish immigrants of the 1980s headed overwhelmingly to London to find work. But by the late 1980s, I was becoming aware of another type of immigrant; the type I call the welfare immigrant. At first I was puzzled when I learned of people leaving Ireland for Manchester or Birmingham, but eventually I understood. If you weren't looking for work, but only looking to swap one welfare system for another, then it made sense to come to the like of Manchester where the cost of living was less than in London and housing was much easier to get.

So welfare immigrants were what I was looking for here at the DSS in Cheetham. I wasn't having much luck on my first day but I would wait all week if I had to. It was late in the day when things began to happen for me. I heard northern Irish accents from among a group of people who went into the DSS. The man was aged about thirty and the woman was a few years younger. These might be worth waiting for. Eventually they came out.

The man was friendly. He was skinny with sharp features and a sharp Belfast accent. He had tattoos. Colourful, professional tattoos of skulls, busty women, devils and stuff like that. Nothing political that I could see. He introduced his girlfriend. She, he said, was from Derry. That meant he was most likely Catholic. The woman had a middle-class voice and appearance. She had no visible tattoos.

We came here, said the man, because her parents didn't like me. She dropped out of Magee College to be with me. But they didn't approve of me because of my background. We're a mixed couple.

So, I figured, she's Protestant and he's Catholic. But I doubted that it was just bigotry that made her parents dislike him. He didn't seem to be the sort of person that you would want your daughter to drop out of college for. It was just too bloody easy for him to blame all his problems on anti-Catholic bigotry.

I asked the woman if she thought it was over religion that her parents didn't like her boyfriend. Och no, she said. They're not bigots but they're wild snobby. (In Derry speech, "wild" means "very".)

I turned to the man again. Were you ever in trouble with the law?

For taking and driving, that's joyriding, when I was younger. The others were for assaults and stupid things with drink.

Two more people joined us. One was a middle-aged man with a London accent and the other was a woman in her late thirties with a Manchester accent. They seemed to be friends with the Irish couple.

I'm from Ireland, said the woman. Interview me. I'm from Clonmel. Have you ever heard of it?

She told me she had come to Manchester when she was twenty. I married an Englishman but he was no good. I need a new man. She put her arms around me and kissed my cheek. There was a smell of drink off her.

Give us one of those cans there, said the Belfast man. The Londoner opened a plastic bag full of tins of beer. He seemed annoyed, or maybe he always had that expression on his face. He was high-coloured and balding with his hair swept across from his temple and greased back over his head. He wore a jacket and tie. The jacket had patches on the elbows. I got the impression from the Londoner that he didn't approve of me. I turned back to the Belfast man.

Where are you from in Belfast?

Tiger's Bay.

That surprised me. If they were a mixed couple and he was from Tiger's Bay, then he was the Protestant and she the Catholic. I had got their religions the wrong way around.

I know Tiger's Bay, I said. All the kerb stones are painted

red, white and blue. And what do you call that tattoo artist has the shop there? Dixie?

The Belfast man seemed pleased and impressed that I knew his home area. You know Dixie? No, not personally. I've just been fascinated by his tattoo studio and the display in the window.

The Clonmel woman had her arms around my neck again. Isn't he lovely? she kept saying. Even though she was a bit drunk, it was still kind of flattering. She wasn't bad-looking and her body felt lovely and warm against mine on what was a cold day.

I was making my mind up, now, about why the Belfast man was here in Manchester.

Do you ever go back to Belfast?

No. I can't.

I'm going to take a guess. You're in Britain because your life was threatened by loyalist paramilitaries.

The man nodded. He took a swig from his can, put it down and undid his pants. He pulled his pants down to his ankles. Both his knees were disfigured. It was a characteristic Protestant assault. The knees were smashed, probably with concrete blocks or with a manhole cover. (The IRA assaults, with bullets through the calf or behind the knee, are easier to cope with medically, although since the ceasefire the previous month, the IRA had taken to using Protestant-style methods, that is, concrete blocks instead of bullets.)

It was the UVF, he said, for anti-social behaviour. The next one I got would have been in the nut.

He didn't seem bothered that his pants were down out on the street. He didn't care if anybody saw him. Like those winos you see piddling at the side of the road.

What's anti-social behaviour?

63

Fighting with my wife. It caused the RUC to be brought into the area. It was all drink.

Don't blame the drink, said the Clonmel woman. My husband always blamed drink and he took my kids away from me, the bastard. The courts were against me because I'm Irish.

I was looking at the Belfast man's knees, trying to get the Clonmel woman's arms out of my way, when the Londoner suddenly smashed his fist into the Clonmel woman's belly. I heard the wind driven from both ends of her body. She doubled over in pain and breathlessness.

Do you wanta fuck him then, do you? You fucking tart. I bought you drink all fucking day, didn't I? Bought drink for fucking all of you. You can all fuck off.

The Londoner turned and walked away. I held the injured woman and sat her down. She fought for breath. He's always the same, she said. He'll be back. The Irish couple agreed. Och, he gets like that, so he does.

They all left. The Belfast man was muttering about the Londoner having gone off with all the drink.

It was a relief when they were gone. I was trying to make sense of what I had just seen. Surely there wasn't a romance between this good-looking Clonmel woman and the middle-aged Londoner who had just beaten her to the ground? And when he beats her, what do her friends say? Och, he gets like that so he does. The beating of a woman seemed to be a routine thing for them. As for the young Derry woman, she was then, and remains to this day, a mystery to me. She didn't seem to be a drinker. What was she thinking of, hanging around Manchester with a crowd like that? God love her mum and dad, the wild snobby ones. They must have been worried sick about her.

A while later the Londoner came back. He was still angry

and now I was the object of his anger. Did you fuck her then? You should've. Buy her drink and she fucks anyone.

The Londoner was snarling into my face. His face was contorted in anger and spittle flecked his lips. This is what women put up with from drunken husbands. I was seeing him the way his Clonmel girlfriend sees him when he's drunk. I needed to get out of here. I can talk my way out of most situations but drunks frighten me. There's no talking to them.

I walked away and the Londoner kept shouting after me. All his abuse concerned the woman. He didn't seem to be angry at me.

I walked back towards the city centre. Drink, I think, is second only to heroin as the drug that can destroy lives. What was the Clonmel woman doing with a man like that? I think the Londoner had it right. Buy her drink and she fucks anyone.

London
Department of Social Security, Hackney;
January 1995

What are you fucking looking at, you black bastard?

She was middle-aged, stout, drunk and Irish. She was abusing the security man, a huge black man, at the social security office.

Why is it that, of all nationalities, the loud-mouth drunk is most likely to be Irish? That's not a rhetorical question on my part. It's one I think there's an answer to that I hope is provided in this book.

There were loads of nationalities here. Leaflets on your welfare rights were available in sixteen languages. These were Arabic, Urdu, Gujrati, Punjabi, Chinese, Turkish, Serbo-Croat,

Somalian and more that I can't remember, including some languages I had never heard of. The place was jammed. People queued at the hatches. Others sat for hours, trying to keep their children quiet, waiting for their ticket number to be called so as to get to an interview in one of the booths.

The Irishwoman kept shouting abuse. I'm not scared of you, yeh black bastard. She had a can of beer in her hand, even though there was a sign up saying that the consumption of alcohol on the premises was prohibited. The security man didn't intervene. I guess he drew on experience and decided that if he stopped looking at her she would stop shouting at him. She did.

Perhaps there were more Irish here. Quiet ones that I hadn't noticed. I decided to wait outside awhile.

The pavement is full of spits. Why do so many people feel the need to come out and spit? (Now, that *is* meant as a rhetorical question.) I go through the day without spitting and I don't feel any the worse for it. But people come out from waiting in the DSS, out to the foyer for a smoke, and then maybe outdoors for a spit.

A middle-aged Londoner came out and spoke to me. Is there a dog around here, mate?

I'm sorry?

A dog. A dog-and-bone.

He put his hand to the side of his face in a telephone gesture. Now I understood. The nearest one was inside the pub at the corner.

A frail old woman laughed along with me at my confusion. Are you Irish? I said I was. I'm Irish, too, she said, in a strong London accent. My father was O'Shaughnessy. Shocker they called me. I used to work for the RAF in Wales during the war and the men called me Shocker. I was wild, yes I was. (She laughed what could be described as a dirty laugh.) But it's all changed now. It's the cars, you see, the white cars. Look.

Shocker took out a notebook. It was filled with dates and times. She explained that these were the occasions over the last several weeks on which she had observed white-coloured cars passing her house. She had told the police but they had done nothing about it.

Shocker was mad.

A West Indian with a woolly hat and a beard was smoking a joint. He turned to me and Shocker. He breathed deeply, then spoke in a West Indian accent. It's hard to convey that accent in print. It goes up and down in pitch and is punctuated with pauses that seem to have nothing to do with the sense of what is being said.

Now, eet's gan. All gan. An-til. Thee next time. You people try smoke it. Eet's good but now. Eet's gan.

Wot's gorn? Shocker sounded impatient.

Thee feeling. Man.

I have doubts about this accent being always genuine here in London. I suspect it's used as a sort of cultural badge, like the woolly hats and the joints. Bob Geldof once described how black Londoners could turn on the West Indian accent at will when they were branding him a racist for not having a sufficient quota of black musicians at his Live Aid gig in Wembley in 1985.

Two young women came out. They were Dubliners. Good. I always seem to get lucky when I meet Dubliners. They were friendly and good-humoured. Giddy, even.

You interviewed us once before, they said. That was in Ballymun at the post office. We're sisters. And you interviewed me at the pawn in Capel Street. I'll meet you in heaven, I will. We're getting on great here, we are. We haven't touched drugs since we came to London.

Is that why you left Dublin? To get off drugs?

That, and to get away from me boyfriend, said one. He was beating me up and he was gambling but I have a new fellah now. He's from London.

He's no good either, said the sister.

He's all right, said the other. He stabbed me once, but he's all right.

They described how they left Dublin. People said our flat was a shooting gallery, that we were letting in junkies. But that was only me brother and his friends. And there was a big crowd came to our landing one night and they knocked. There was two men and two women at the door and they told us we were going to be put out if we didn't stop leaving in the junkies. After that they came one night and they broke up the place. They broke the bathroom and the toilet pot and all and they gave me brother a few digs and they told him he'd get a worse hiding the next time. So we came to England and it was great. We were in a squat first but we have a flat now.

She pointed to some tower blocks the other side of the main road.

And are you staying away from drugs?

Ah, yeah. It was the best thing we ever done, to come here. There's drugs around, but you're not with your friends here. We're much better. We've had no trouble with the law. We're here three months now and I haven't even been *arrested* since we got here.

Were you in a lot of trouble in Dublin?

An awful lot, said one. An awful lot of trouble, we were.

She got more serious, remembering the bad times. She asked me to turn off the tape-recorder. It was what I had to do for drugs, you know? I mean not just robbing.

You mean prostitution?

She nodded. The worst was when I got flush, is that what you call it? It's from sex you get it. You'd be scratching, you know? And I had all discharge in me knickers. Thrush. That's what it was. I'm still going to the hospital about it here.

I asked them how they got on with the blacks and all the other races here. It's all right, they said. Didn't bother them. What about the woman in the DSS who was shouting abuse at the security man?

Ah, the knacker? Don't mind her. She's always here. There's loads of knackers come here.

It surprised me to learn that the drunk woman was a traveller. Most traveller women I have met are non-drinkers.

A scrawny, scruffy man aged about forty approached me. He was wearing a dark blue, peaked cap with a crossed swords crest on it in the style of the old American cavalry. I'll call him General Custer. He was rough-looking. I think he had a broken nose. There were old scars on his chin and neck. General Custer turned out to be a nuisance whom I couldn't shake off for the next several days.

Custer had a rural, southern Irish accent of some sort with a strong overlay of London. He hadn't been home for years. He was a know-all. I understand the system here. You have to understand the system for the Irish coming over. Custer was the hero of all his stories, how he stood up to the DSS, sorted them out. I filled a few minutes of tape with his ramblings. I suspected he had a past in Ireland that he was running from. A wife and kids maybe. Or perhaps drink-related crime. But General Custer would say nothing interesting.

A middle-aged man approached me and reminded me that I had met him once before in Limerick. He was a traveller. I had interviewed some of his relatives at the Moyross estate. I asked how they were doing now? All back in England, it turned out. In Birmingham, for the most part.

I remembered that Limerick programme. I went to the Glenagross area of Moyross and knocked on the doors of the inhabited houses. Over sixty houses had been burned down by vandals. I interviewed that man's brother who praised the police in Limerick for their handling of the glue-sniffing problem. He also said that the Moyross community police (co*new*nity police, he called them, finding the big word difficult) were much better than the gardai before them who used to stop and search his eldest son whenever they saw him carrying anything, anywhere.

And had this Limerick man at the DSS been living long in England? He was here most of his life, he told me. He was in the British Army when he was younger.

This answer interested me. I know that Irish travellers often used to join the British Army. Maybe they still do. In Navan, a few months before, I had interviewed a middle-aged traveller woman at the health board office who told me that her father and uncles had all been British soldiers. Likewise, in Cork in 1994, in a caravan on the halting site high on the hill of Knocknaheeny, I interviewed a Mrs Clarke who told me that when she was young, her family moved to England and her father became a British soldier. And did he mind giving up his way of life in a caravan? Indeed, we hadn't a caravan, said Mrs Clarke. We had a jinnet and cart and a tent. Sometimes the farmers would let us sleep in their sheds when we were working on the farms. And why did your father not join the Irish army? Because, she said, the Irish army had no meas for the travellers.

Meas (the pronounciation is mass, the spelling given here is my own guess) is a traveller word which means love or esteem. So travellers found themselves better accepted in the

British army than in the Irish one. That makes sense to me. Traditionally, poor men became soldiers. But poor travellers, such as Mrs Clarke's father, found even this work option cut off to them. Therefore they joined the British Army where they would be considered to be simply Irishmen, rather than travellers.

I would like to have asked this Limerick man about his army days but we were interrupted by noise from the foyer of the DSS. The security man was escorting the middle-aged Irishwoman out, the one who had been doing all the shouting earlier. She was holding her giro in her hand and now she was being got rid off. She shouted to the man I was talking to, whom she obviously knew. He went over and took her off the security man's hands and encouraged her to come away quietly. They may have been husband and wife. I don't know.

General Custer was driving me mad. You need to tell the politicians to cop on, driving about in all their big cars and all. Put that in your radio programme. I told Custer I had to go and buy batteries for my tape-recorder.

I got lunch in one of those nice places they call working-men's cafes that you find in working-class areas of British cities. They're good value and the staff always seem to be cheerful and friendly. I was enjoying Hackney. People are nice in the shops, too. They reminded me of New Yorkers, the way they seem to take a pride in serving you. If I was a working-class Londoner I think I would resent the *Eastenders* soap opera on television. That programme is made up of a succession of rows between its characters. All being straight wiv each uvver, right? That's not what working-class London is like.

I was reading the paper, sitting having a cup of tea after lunch when I looked up to find General Custer standing in

71

front of me. Oh, no. Does this guy never give up? I bought Custer a cup of tea and endured him a while longer. The police were after him, he told me, because this girl said he hit her. She was staying with him. She was a teenager from Scotland and he put her up because she needed to understand how the system worked here. Then after about a week we had a row and I told her I wasn't taking any shit from anyone, man or woman.

I knew General Custer was unstable. Probably very nasty in certain circumstances. Like with a vulnerable teenage runaway. I went back to work.

There's a colony of young people from Portlaoise in Hackney. They were all from the area of town known as the White City which is a welfare ghetto with all white-painted houses. White City is not its official name but Portlaoise people call it that under their breath. It's considered to be a bad address.

One young Portlaoise woman was living in a squat. It's easy to squat here, she said. She started off living with other people from Mar'boro, as she called it, and now she was in with two black London girls. She left Mar'boro because she didn't like her mum's boyfriend. She was working now, in London, whereas nobody in Mar'boro would give her a job because she was from the White City.

(Mar'boro is an old name for Portlaoise that is still sometimes used by people from that town and from the surrounding countryside of Co Laois. Portlaoise was once called Maryborough and Co Laois was called Queen's County.)

A young Portlaoise man explained that he signs on here and also, with his brother's birth cert, he signs on in Lisson Grove. He was working, too. He hadn't been home to

Mar'boro for five years. He left when he was sixteen because the law was after him.

His story about signing on twice was familiar to me from my years attending DSS offices in London. I think most Irish people who sign on in London are signing on fraudulently. Most sign only once but nearly everybody is working black. It's the only way to live. If you were to give up your unemployment pay you would also lose your rent allowance. So young Irish people in London, like the young people you meet here from all over Britain, are signing on while working in low-paid, dead-end jobs. That way, you can survive.

The next day at the Hackney DSS I met a middle-aged Dublin man who wore shabby clothes. He spoke to me but said he wouldn't speak to RTE, as he put it, because it would embarrass his two brothers back home if he was heard on the radio. He named two brothers who were in prominent jobs in Dublin, in one case, on the board of a semi-state company. I didn't know the man's brothers personally but I had heard of both of them. He was the black sheep. They both had good jobs but he was better off in London because he had let the family down. He gave me a smile and shook my hand and left.

A Belfast man, aged about thirty-five, with black curly hair and a ready smile, was pleased to meet me. He was from Turf Lodge. He did time for armed robbery in Belfast. The initials IRA were in blue ink on his wrist. Was the robbery an IRA job? No, it wasn't, he laughed. Don't mind my hand. I did that when I was a youngster and had no sense.

The Belfast man had come to London, he told me, to escape from the Brits and from everyone else who was giving him trouble after he came out of prison. Who was giving you trouble? Everyone else, he said. Everyone. There's boys want you to do jobs, you know? (Boys means men in Belfast.) They're coming saying they need a driver for a job and I'm

73

telling them no, I don't do that any more. I'd be back in prison now if I was still in Belfast.

I thought I had a clear enough picture of the Belfast man as a former criminal trying to go straight when he started asking me about Dublin and he showed an alarming familiarity with a Dublin criminal gang. He asked after a certain middle-aged lesbian whose lover was the sister of one of Dublin's most notorious criminals of the 1980s. If he knew that lesbian he was quite likely once involved in drugs. I think he was telling me the truth when he said he left Belfast because he was in trouble with everyone. That meant criminals and perhaps paramilitaries as well as the law.

General Custer turned up and he was drunk. He was nasty, too. Well hello Mr RTE. I hope you had a good night's sleep in your luxury hotel. You haven't a clue about how people like us live. And you asked me all the wrong questions yesterday. If you put that on the radio, I'll fucking kill you. I have friends in this town.

I assured Custer that I wouldn't put what he said the day before on the radio. He needn't have worried about that. I take a pride in my work. I could take no more of General Custer. I said goodbye. I was finished work for the day.

I could understand, now, how General Custer got his scars and his broken nose. He was a man with a bad attitude and, no doubt, he got himself into fights. The only good thing about him was that he wasn't big. He was only big enough to frighten runaway teenage girls.

Kilburn, later that week

Hackney had been interesting but I can't resist Kilburn. I had just a few hours left before getting the flight back to Dublin that afternoon. It was wet and windy this morning. I stood outside the DSS at Dyne Road but soon gave up trying to work. I had a good week's work behind me and I decided I deserved a drink.

I went into one of Kilburn's pubs. I was sitting at the bar when two young men came in and approached me. They were Dubliners. You're the chap who does the surveys, one of them said to me. The surveys for the radio. You interviewed me ma once in Ballyfermot.

That's right, I said. We're just off the bus, they told me. We came over from Dublin last night. We're trying to find our mate. His ma in Ballyfermot is after dying and nobody knows where he is. Do you know where Dublin fellahs drink around here?

I said I didn't but I would try to find out. The lads sat down at a table and ordered soup and sandwiches. I asked the barman if he knew of any Dublin pub in Kilburn. The barman was a big fellow with a rural accent. He was rude. I don't know where Dubliners drink but they don't drink here.

I finished my pint and was getting ready to leave when the barman went over to the table where the Dublin lads were sitting and opened the window next to them, causing the wind and rain to blow in on top of them.

The lads got the message and realised they weren't welcome. They left along with me. They had been polite at all times but they were treated rudely because they were from Dublin. That barman's a bastard, they said. They were right. He was an ignorant, culchie bastard.

I'll return, now, to something I said earlier. I said I would have a go at explaining why loud-mouth drunks at welfare offices are most likely Irish. If I haven't already answered that question implicitly in this book then I need to answer it explicitly now.

Irish people on the welfare in Britain are refugees. All of them are in some sense on the run from Ireland. At British DSS offices over the years, I have met Irish jobless people, homeless people, travellers, alcoholics, drug addicts, mentally ill people, orphans and other people brought up in care, people wanted by the police in Ireland, ex-prisoners, sexually-abused people and sex abusers, police-informers, wife-beaters and beaten wives, unmarried mothers, women who have come to England for an abortion and, from Northern Ireland, all or most of these categories along with joyriders, drug-dealers and people who might be none of the above but who are on the run from the paramilitaries of one or other religion. You learn a lot about Ireland through standing at a British welfare office.

Britain takes our unwanted people. Nobody else does. When I think of all the Irish people I have ever met at British welfare offices, I would say that very few or none would qualify for entry to the USA. The Americans are supposed to love us but, in reality, they are fussy about who they let in. Britain, not America, is the place of refuge for unwanted Irish people.

Drug addicts are just the latest category of unwanted people whom we export to Britain. There is all-party political support now for getting as many of our junkies as possible to go to England. Alleged dealers, which includes most junkies, are being thrown out of their homes, either by vigilantes or by the local authorities. At time of writing, plans are underway to prevent these evicted people from getting rent allowance if they try to move into private flats. So where are they to go? Many sleep rough around Dublin. Others go to England.

We send our sinners to England. As a child at school in Ireland, I quickly learned that England, where I came from, was the second most wicked country in the world. Ireland regarded itself as a more virtuous country than England. I think probably most emergent nationalist countries have that view of themselves vis-à-vis the old colonial power. As a virtuous country we didn't have room for sinners. (The most wicked country in the world, in case you don't know, was Russia.)

Forced emigration to England has always been a form of social cleansing of Ireland. We get rid of our worst, or people who are judged to be our worst. So after generations of social cleansing through emigration it should be no surprise that our worst people are in England. The loud-mouth drunk at the welfare office is most likely Irish.

Next time you're in London, take a walk down Kilburn High Road of an evening. See all those drunks sitting around, growling? They look suspiciously like what some people tell me is a negative stereotype of the Irish in Britain. They are the people who have been forced to go to England because they are failed Irish people. At least, in England, they can fail in a kind of privacy.

Liverpool
Department of Social Security, Toxteth;
February 1995

Of all the winos who hung around the DSS, the joke-teller was the most pathetic. He was aged about fifty. His jokes were long and rambling. Jokes were his only way of speaking with people. No real conversation. No two-way exchange between one person and another. Just his bloody jokes that let him demand your attention for a few minutes until you could get back to ignoring him again.

My mind wandered whenever he cornered me with one of his stories. I could never follow him. I was too busy noticing his blood-shot eyes and avoiding the stink from his breath. But I would know when he'd reached the punch-line because he would finish speaking and look at me with wide-eyed expectation. That would be the moment when I had to feign laughter.

There was no reason to upset the poor fool and plenty of reason not to. I was in wino territory here. It was the foyer of the DSS and the winos were using it, same as I was, to stay in from the cold and the rain. I also wanted to use the foyer to conduct interviews with any Irish people I might meet here. The DSS staff would probably put me out if they noticed me with the microphone so the last thing I needed to do was to draw attention to myself by having a row with one of the winos.

The rain eased off and I took my chances outside for a while. A man aged about forty walked up to me and, in a strong local accent, said something to me about a watch. I'm sorry, I said, I don't have a watch but I think it's about midday. He pulled a handful of watches from his coat pocket. No, he said, I'm asking if you want to buy a watch?

The Liverpool accent, or Scouse, is unique. The end of each sentence goes up in pitch and in emphasis, making it different from all other accents of the north of England.

The watch-seller was sober and seemed friendly. I explained that I was a journalist looking for Irish people. The watch-seller brightened up. The pitch of his voice varied even more.

You're Irish! Me best mate, e's Irish! 'E was in prison in Ireland. 'E was in the IRA or something. 'E did time for attempted *meer*dah. 'Ere 'e comes now.

The man's friend was aged about forty-five. He was tall

and lean with long dark hair and a long moustache. His coat was a bit tatty, his shoes also, but his hair and moustache were carefully-groomed. He was friendly and pleased to talk to me.

He had a northern Irish accent. He told me where he was from, a town in Antrim. (It surprised me that he should be from that town. It was mainly Protestant. Not a likely place for an IRA man to come from.)

The Antrim man told me he was four years in Liverpool. He liked it here but there was a big problem with drugs. We're worried for our son, or my girlfriend's son, I should say. We had never heard of smack or crack when we lived in Belfast. He wouldn't go back, though.

I took his point about drugs. I had already seen plenty of junkies at the DSS that morning. You would never see that in a Belfast DSS. There's no heroin in Belfast. But Liverpool's drug problem looks as bad as that of Dublin.

The Antrim man had tattoos on his hands. I asked if I could see them and he held his hands out for me. The tattoos were amateur blue ink jobs. Ulster, tartan, 1690 and, most tellingly of all, UDA. He told me he put them on when he was sixteen and regretted it now. But it's not so bad here because English people don't understand these tattoos. The English haven't a clue, he said. The tattoos don't get you into fights here like they do in Northern Ireland.

I felt that there was a strong reason why this man had come to England. A life and death matter, perhaps. I didn't let on that I knew about his prison sentence. I asked if he was ever a member of the UDA and he said no. Were you ever in prison? He shrugged his shoulders. He chose not to be drawn.

A woman came out of the DSS and called out to the Antrim man. Are you coming? She had a Belfast accent. She was gorgeous-looking and, like the man, she was careful about her appearance. The man said goodbye to me. I knew there was a story there but I wasn't going to learn what it was. As it turned out, that would take another two days. For today, I got back to looking for more Irish people coming out of the DSS.

Irish people have white skin. That distinguishes them from maybe half of the callers at this DSS in Toxteth. There are lots of blacks and Asians here. Of the whites, if I thought a person might be Irish, I would try to get them to speak, ask the time maybe, then listen for the accent. It started to rain again. I went back in to brave the winos.

The joke-teller had another one for me. This was one I actually remember. A British lorry driver was getting hassle in Germany so he told those Germans that the last time he unloaded his vehicle in their country it took him only two minutes. And vot vere you driving? A Lancaster fucking bomber. The joke was a lot longer than that but I've given you the punch-line.

There are always mad people at social security offices. A middle-aged West Indian woman was complaining to anyone who would listen. She was small and stout with a head-scarf and lots of jewelry. They are after me. I've been to the police, do you see?

She held up a heavy, brown paper envelope in front of my face. It had arrived in the post that morning, she said. They want to kill me. And now this. She held up another envelope, this time from the DSS. She explained about the DSS letter and she didn't seem to be mad after all. I understood her story.

She was summoned to the social welfare office because a report had been received that she had gone to Trinidad to see her daughter, who was studying medicine there. While she was allegedly away, another person had been collecting income support in her name. It's not true, she said. She had to see the authorities today to satisfy them that nobody claimed money in her name except her. It wasn't the first time, she told me, that reports had gone in against her. She was the victim of a hate campaign. Was that a racial thing?

No. Not from white people. From black people. They don't like me. They don't like my daughter because she's too clever. See what I got in the post today? I'll show you.

She unwrapped the brown paper parcel and pulled a plastic bag from inside. I braced myself to see something vile. It turned out to be something fairly harmless-looking, at least at first sight. It was a child's doll. A dark-skinned doll with black hair. The doll's blouse was stained red and a pin had been forced into its chest. It's supposed to be me, she said. It's a voodoo doll.

I didn't know what to say. Really? Does that frighten you?

She laughed derisively. No, it wasn't a real voodoo doll. A real voodoo doll would have needed a part of her hair or some part of her clothing attached to it for the black magic to work. She was still upset by it, though. She had brought it to the local police around the corner at Admiral Road.

The next day at the DSS, I was stuck with the joke-teller again. He was going on with some story about black women's tits when a man came in and, in a strong west of Ireland accent, greeted the other winos. How's the men? This fellow was a candidate for interview.

I got past the joke-teller and introduced myself to the new arrival. You're from RTE? You're not! And d'you know Gay Byrne? Patrick's my name. Patrick was delighted to talk.

Patrick was a big man with snowy white hair and a reddish face. He was from Mayo. He comes here every day, he told me, to meet his mates. They sit here and drink sherry. He left Claremorris when he was sixteen. He was thirty-eight now. (I would have guessed his age at more than that.) I was always a black sheep, he said. To tell you the truth, I was always fond of drink.

Patrick listed the British prisons he had done time in. It was for Section 47s. What's a Section 47, Patrick? Giving fellahs a slap.

Patrick was a big man. What he called a slap would be serious.

Patrick was facing more charges. Was that more Section 47s? No, he said. 'Twas for robbing the lead off a roof. I do the scrap, too.

Patrick was friendly and, for the moment at least, sober. But I could see how he might get himself into trouble. He talked to everybody and was cheeky. One of the winos saw my microphone and told me to leave Patrick alone because he was his friend. Patrick told him to cop on to himself. I could see a Section 47 coming. I got out.

I walked around Toxteth awhile. Toxteth is interesting. It's all local authority flats and houses and they're well-maintained, proving to me once again that there is nothing wrong with high-intensity housing so long as it's well looked after and the people there aren't all left jobless. Toxteth looks as good as any Housing Executive estate in Northern Ireland, and Northern Ireland has the best local authority housing anywhere in the UK. Whether it be in Belfast or Liverpool, rioting pays dividends.

Toxteth is racially-mixed. There are whites, blacks, Asians and Afro-Caribbeans. The little shops, of which there are many, are all run by Asians. But the Asians aren't just a lower middle-class. There's plenty of them at the DSS, too.

Back at the DSS a Dublin man I met told me he suffered from mental illness. It had been diagnosed as post-traumatic stress syndrome, following his two tours of duty in Lebanon.

He became depressed, left the army and turned to drug abuse. Three years ago, Liverpool was his escape from the Dublin drug scene. He kept his own company here and was able to stay off drugs. He liked Liverpool. He played Irish music in a pub in town. That made him some money. He hoped that later this year he would be well enough to go back to Ireland and face his family again.

A young Liverpool man told me about heroin. His accent was Scouse but his story sounded just like the stories of countless addicts I have interviewed in Dublin over the years. A life of crime, prison and, for his family, heartbreak. He had cousins in Dublin who were also addicts. But he stayed away from crack. The drug problem is worse in Liverpool than in Dublin, he told me, because of crack cocaine. He explained that a heroin addict wakes up, steals something and, once he gets his fix, his craving is satisfied for most of the day. But a crack addict gets his fix, gets a massive high, and then suffers a corresponding low within hours. The crack addict steals again to turn on again. A crackhead is worse than a smackhead, he said.

Since that interview, I have tried to learn more about crack cocaine. It's cocaine that's mixed with baking soda and water and then boiled. In this form it can be smoked, rather than snorted. Smoking it causes it to be absorbed by the lungs which makes it go more efficiently to the brain. The result is a quicker, more intense drug experience which, as the Scouser told me, leads to an equally sudden low which in turn causes the user to want to take crack once again. So crack is more addictive than its parent drug, cocaine, because of the intense cycle of use that it engenders.

Crack is a poor person's drug, a drug of the ghetto. Crack is cheap because a small amount of cocaine provides a lot of crack. In New York, reputed to be the crack capital of the world, an ounce of cocaine costing $1000 is typically rendered into one thousand vials of crack costing $5 each. Crack was the marketing solution designed by cocaine merchants to sell their product to the poor. Cocaine remains a drug of the middle-class and most regular cocaine users choose not to take their drug in the form of crack.

In Ireland, crack use is rare. I have only twice interviewed people who have smoked crack. Both were junkies, that is, heroin addicts, who had tried crack only once. Cocaine is available in Ireland and is used by rich people. Remember Ben Dunne? Converting cocaine to crack, so as to be able to smoke it, is a simple operation that you can learn about on the Internet. So it's not a question of whether or not crack ever "comes in" to Ireland. Cocaine is here, so crack is here too.

I hope crack use never becomes widespread in Ireland but, if crack does catch on, there's not much that anybody will be able to do about it.

Crack, in itself, doesn't cause people to go crazy or induce them to commit crimes, any more than heroin does. In New York, most crack-related murders are the result of dealer disputes. And, of course, crack-users steal to feed their habit, as junkies do.

Bad as crack is, it's less addictive than heroin is and it doesn't lead to death as surely as heroin does. Also, the use of crack doesn't spread the Aids virus as the use of heroin does. Since the advent of Aids in the 1980s, heroin is killing more efficiently than it has ever done before. Most junkies that I have known are dead. On balance, I think the Scouser had it wrong. A smackhead is worse than a crackhead.

Day three in Liverpool and it was the first day it wasn't raining. I walked from my hotel at Lime Street in the city centre to Toxteth where I was working. It's a nice walk. It takes about half an hour. The Mersey estuary is on your right and you pass both cathedrals on your left. The first cathedral is the modern one, a sort of conical, gasometer-looking thing that Scousers call the Wigwam. The next one is the huge hulk that is Liverpool Cathedral, built early in the 20th-century.

I reached the DSS and stood outside. A woman walked up to me. It was the glamorous Belfast woman I had seen two days earlier. I was hoping you'd turn up, she said. You interviewed my partner. The man from Antrim. There was something she wanted to say to me.

She was in Liverpool because she had to be here. She was from a Protestant area of Belfast and had given information against loyalist paramilitaries who had beaten her and her son. She was angry because she still couldn't go home. The ceasefire hadn't lifted the death-threat hanging over her. She could never go home to see her mother. She was a refugee in England, like so many other Irish people who are waiting for the paramilitaries, at their own convenience, to lift the banishment orders that they have issued. The ceasefire means nothing to me, she said. There's no peace for us.

She lifted a sleeve and showed me one of her elbows. It was an injury typical of the sort I had seen many times before in Belfast. The victim is held on the ground and a steel manhole cover or, as in this case, a baseball bat, is smashed into the victim's limbs. The elbow or knee is permanently disfigured. This woman had a steel plate in her arm, she told me, to replace what was her elbow. And I can never wear a skirt now, she said. They had done her knees, too.

I appreciated her point about not wearing a skirt. She was an attractive woman and took pride in her appearance. I bet she used to look good in a skirt.

You gave the RUC the names of the men who beat you

up. That's a death sentence. Why did you do it? Could you not have done what everybody else does and say that they wore masks and that you didn't know who they were?

I'll tell you why they beat us. The time they beat my son, it was drugs. For me, it was because they said I had an affair. My husband was in the paramilitaries and you don't have an affair when you're married to a man like that.

And were you having an affair?

Yes, I was. You've met the man.

So you're telling me it was your husband who sent the gang to beat you?

No. I'm telling you, the one with the baseball bat, that was my husband.

Two winos approached us. One was the joke-teller. The other was a middle-aged, red-faced man with white bristles on his chin. The bristly one stuck his face against mine and snarled at me. I'm from Limavady, and what fucking about it? I held my breath against the stink from his. My glamorous Belfast friend said goodbye and left.

So you're from Limavady, I said, trying to force a smile. I know Limavady, it's in Co Derry.

The bristly one's face contorted and he jabbed his finger into my chest. Co *London*derry, he roared, and don't you forget it.

The joke-teller told the Limavady man to leave me alone. He's all right, he is, said the joke-teller. So my days of putting up with jokes had paid off. The joke-teller was on my side.

I said goodbye to the men and left. I was happy with the work I had done in Liverpool. I was pleased with my interview with the Belfast woman and now I was going home. It had been a long three days. I was sick of the sight of that DSS.

But the joke-teller wasn't finished. He followed me down

the road and I ducked into a corner shop. He waited outside. No doubt, the Pakistani running the shop knew the joke-teller and wouldn't allow him in.

I had to go back out and face the joke-teller. Mate, he said, in a pleading voice. He gripped my hand. If I got him a bottle of sherry he would give me a story for my radio programme, the like of which I had never heard before. I told him I was sorry, but I wouldn't buy him a drink. I didn't bother saying to him that his voice was so slurred that there would be no point in recording anything he said, anyway.

But mate, just one bottle. You can get it in Safeways. He wouldn't let go. I was going to hear his story anyway.

The joke-teller's wife and daughter lived in Ireland. In Dublin, he thought, but he wasn't sure. He hadn't seen either of them for years. He was in prison a lot of the time and he lost touch.

Why do you think they're in Ireland?

Cos she left me for an Irishman, a Dublin chap. He met her here and he took her away from me. And I haven't seen my daughter, my own daughter, for years. Years.

His grip on my hand was hurting me now. He was crying. I felt sorry for him but I was on his wife's side. Maybe she left him because of his drinking and perhaps violence or whatever it was he went to prison for. Or maybe she left him because of his boring bloody jokes. There's only so much you could take of a man like that.

Just a bottle of sherry, mate. One like this. He held up his now-empty bottle. Five pound fifty in Safeways.

What does it matter? I thought. Drink is all he has in life. I went into Safeways and bought him the sherry. It was his lucky day.

I walked back towards the city centre where I was staying. Later that night, I phoned Deirdre in Dublin. She had good news. She had got a job as an advertising salesperson with the *Sunday Tribune.* Well done, Deirdre. For months you made a brave effort selling life insurance, a job I would put on a level with selling encyclopedias at doors, and now, at last, you've got something better. You've worked hard and you deserve the break. Pity we can't go out to celebrate. I'll see you in Dublin tomorrow.

I had to celebrate on my own. I crossed to Lime Street station and gave a taxi-man the name of the pub that my soldier-interviewee from the day before told me that he sometimes played music in. Is that the bikers' pub, mate? the driver asked. That surprised me. I decided to go there anyway.

We reached the pub I was looking for. It was a small place down a back street in the city centre. It was full of bikers. These are big, hairy men, in their thirties and forties, with fat bellies and tattoos and leather clothes. I sat at the bar.

I got talking with a man about my own age who was sitting at the bar drinking a half-pint of Guinness. A half one, he told me, because he was going to work soon. He was a nurse in a city hospital casualty unit and was going on duty at midnight.

I would say that can be a rough job, I said. Do you see a lot of drugs?

Drugs aren't the problem, mate. We call the wards after brands of beer. The Carling Ward, the Furstenberg Ward. Take last week. Some lads decided to ride their motor-bikes along a wall, which they did, then they went to the pub, then they thought it would be interesting to do the wall thing again after the pub.

The nurse raised his hands in a shrug, as if to say, need I say more?

We talked some more. I told the nurse about the work I

had done that week and the uilleann piper I met. Yes, he said, this is an Irish music pub and it's a bikers' pub and it's a gay pub.

A couple of pints later I was getting up to leave when one of the bikers came up behind me. He put his big, hairy arms around me and slipped his hands down the front of my shirt. What a nice bottom you've got. Tell me, do you *pump* here often?

He was thrusting his hips behind me. The nurse intervened. Mike, stop. (Mike wasn't the name but I'll use it for the purpose of this story.) Leave him alone, Mike. He's straight.

Well if he's straight, what's he doing with *you*?

Mike kept pumping as he spoke.

Mike, this bloke's a journalist. He works for Irish radio.

The nurse's words had a dramatic effect on Mike. He looked shocked. He stopped thrusting his crotch into my arse.

The nurse pressed home his advantage. He told Mike that he should do an interview with me some time. Mike works at the Department of Irish Studies at the University. His grandmother was Irish. He met your president recently, Mary Robinson.

I remembered the occasion. President Robinson was in Liverpool to meet the Irish studies lot. So I had just met a part of the Diaspora. I had been nearly buggered by it.

Mike left us. He's all right, said the nurse. He meant no harm.

And people wonder why I avoid academics.

Chapter Four

WOMEN AND PRISON

Cork Prison;
Christmas Week, 1995

A lot of IRA prisoners were being let out of Portlaoise Prison for Christmas. I had to get a programme on the air for 30 December, so I decided to go to Cork Prison to see how the Christmas temporary release programme was being applied to ordinary criminals of the type that we weren't hearing about on the news. Who was, or wasn't, being let out?

It was two days after Christmas Day and the place was busy. There were taxis coming and going and lots of cars and travellers' vans were parked outside the prison.

A well-dressed woman came out. She agreed to talk to me. She had a middle-class voice, or, at least, a voice that was socially a step away from most of the voices here. Most prisoners here come from the poorest parts of Cork city.

Her son was in for joyriding. One person had been injured but fortunately, was now recovered. He had been in trouble for taking cars even before the accident. It was drink and bad company, she said. For the first few months after her son was sent to prison, she had told the neighbours that her son was away in Dublin studying but eventually she realised she was fooling nobody with this story.

Her tone was resolute. He has to pay for what he's done. He was crying last time, mammy get me out, but I told him to be done with his crying same as I'm finished with crying, too. He doesn't like using a potty to go to the toilet in but I told him he should have thought of all of that before he went taking cars. I'm the only one of the family that comes to see him. My husband won't come near him. He says he still loves him but he can't come here because it would kill him. Her voice dropped as she repeated the words, it would kill him. When this is over, I told him, my brother in England will give him a job. He can't stay here. Nobody will give him a job here any more.

What about Christmas release? Did you apply?

There was no point applying, she said, because she was told he was not long enough into his sentence. But I didn't want him home. He's caused enough upset. This is the place for him now.

My interviewee looked past me at three young men who were coming out of the prison gates. There's lovely boys for you there. Oh, lovely boys. (Think of this in a middle-class Cork accent. Lovely boys.) See now if they'll talk to you. I'll be on my way.

I knew what she meant. The young men were scruffy and scrawny with blue ink tattoos on their fingers. They looked typical of the young criminals who come from the poorest parts of the city. Lovely boys.

The lovely boys were friendly. They were from Mayfield and they remembered me from work I did on drugs in that area. We were just in the prison to see our mate. He was in for setting fire to houses and flats. He was mad with drink at the time. But it was wrong he was in there because he only set fire to one of the houses but he got blamed on the whole lot.

One of the lovely boys was forthright about drink and the problems it caused. You think you're great with drink on you. You do anything. But then you don't feel so great about it the next day. The guards knew it with me. They told me, without drink, you're a gutless little cunt. They were right. I've stopped drinking now. I just stick to my bit of blow (cannabis).

They were getting some blow in to their friend in prison, too. Last year we were throwing tennis balls full of the stuff over the prison walls. But the prison is wide to that now. They've covered in the yard. We still gets the stuff in to him, though, whenever we sees him, like, cos he's our mate.

("Wide to" is a Cork expression that means to be aware of. "Gets" and "sees" are present tense constructions in Cork working-class speech, used when the action described is an ongoing or habitual occurrence. Working-class or regional grammar tends to be more complex than the grammar of standard English.)

Do the prison authorities know that you're getting drugs in?

Well they must know, like. 'Twould be kind of hard to have a joint without anyone knowing.

That made sense when I thought about it. A junkie could be shooting up in his cell in Mountjoy without anyone noticing, but a cannabis smoker is going to be obvious to the whole landing and beyond. I suppose the prison authorities in Cork are not too bothered by dope going in but they have succeeded in keeping heroin out by having a policy of sending no junkies to Cork Prison. Good thinking.

I liked the lovely boys. I interviewed plenty more lovely boys that day and their girlfriends and mothers. People of that social class tend to be friendly and candid and therefore easy to interview. I met a good few travellers too, but these aren't easy to get an interview with. Even if they're friendly, they're rarely candid. Most prisoners here are either lovely boys or travellers. It was in the afternoon that I met a visitor for a different type of prisoner.

She was aged about forty, well-dressed and attractive with a friendly manner. She had driven here from Waterford to see her husband, as she does every week. She was feeling okay now, she said. It's on the way in to see him that her heart thumps and she feels she can't breathe. It's hard for her to get here because she has her children to look after and now, since he's gone inside, a business to run by herself. She was sad that he hadn't been let out over Christmas. Last year, they knew he would have to stay in but she was expecting he might get out this year, if only for a few hours.

I was trying to figure out what he was in for. Clearly, it was a long sentence. He wasn't an underclass criminal of the lovely boy sort. He was a businessman.

Was he ever in prison before?

No.

May I ask you, please, the kind of offence he's in for?

It was a driving thing. He was drinking and he drove the company van. There was an accident.

Was anyone hurt?

One person did die, yes.

I didn't know what to say next, but I had to try something. That must be very hard on both of you?

He said first that he didn't want to live any more, that he wished he had died at the time, but he wasn't even hurt. He's had a long time now to think about it. He's more calm than I am now. It's hard, though, at Christmas. Hard on everyone. I bring flowers to the grave for him because he asks me to. I don't tell anyone who they're from, though.

Are you looking forward to when he gets out?

Very much so. It's what he lives for now, to see me and the kids again.

After we said goodbye, I couldn't get that woman off my mind. Even now I'm shaken as I remember her story. She was suffering on the outside and her husband had to think long and hard on the inside about the person whose death he was involved in. He wasn't done paying the price. He had more years to suffer yet. There was an anti-drink driving campaign running that Christmas. Drinking and driving wrecks lives. You'd better believe it.

I think that man should have got Christmas release, even for the few hours that his wife wanted. He was hardly going to abscond or go drinking and driving again. And he couldn't be regarded as being a danger to the public while he was out. The IRA were being let out of Portlaoise, and getting early release, without ever having to give a commitment that they wouldn't rob banks or shoot gardai. So why should they be let out while the drunk driver was not? The only explanation from the Minister for Justice was that the release of the IRA was designed to "deepen the peace process".

I don't understand the decisions that are taken by the Department of Justice. If there are any guidelines in existence about the granting of Christmas temporary release, I think we should be allowed to know what they are.

Crumlin Road Prison, Belfast;
February 1996

This would be my last ever visit to this prison in Belfast. It was due to close for good in another few weeks. It had been in service as a prison since the previous century. Now the prisoners were being transferred to the more modern

Magherberry (pronounced ma*gab*ry) Prison out in the countryside.

That was bad news for me. I had once tried, without success, to interview prison visitors outside Magherberry. I couldn't manage it because of the busy-bodies, that is, third parties who tried to stop me talking to people.

At Magherberry, the busy-bodies are known as Quakers. The car park for visitors is at the outer perimeter of the prison compound, about a quarter mile from the gates of the prison building. That leaves a long distance for visitors to cover to get to the prison. The prison is in an exposed, windswept area on the east side of Lough Neagh.

Some time back, the Quakers got the idea of running a courtesy bus from the car park to the prison. They also run a cafe at the car park where people can wait for the bus. Unlike Crumlin Road, where the prison gate leads straight onto the public street, at Magherberry, the only practical place to try to interview people would be at that cafe. That meant asking permission of the Quakers to be allowed to ask people if they wanted to talk to me.

I hate asking third parties for anything. Third parties suffer from a condition that I call social worker syndrome, that is, a condition which makes the third party believe that a person, particularly a poor person, must never be allowed to answer for himself/herself without the third party being there to supervise. It's not just social workers who suffer from social worker syndrome. It affects all middle-class professionals who deal with poor people. But social workers have it the worst.

I phoned the Quakers at their Belfast HQ and explained who I was and what I wanted to do. The answer was as I thought it would be. No. We have a policy of protecting people's privacy from media intrusion. I didn't argue. There's no point. So here we had a prison full of terrorists and murderers but the Quakers were going to protect their visitors and supporters from me. A classic case of social worker syndrome.

So, when I heard that Crumlin Road Prison was closing down I decided I should make one last radio programme outside its gates. I've done well here over the years. This would be my fifth, and final, programme from Crumlin Road Prison.

The prison is opposite the Court House, which is a building you will have seen a lot of in the news bulletins of the last quarter century. Downhill from the prison is the Mater Hospital and the city centre. Uphill is the road out of Belfast in the direction of Divis Mountain and the town of Crumlin.

I like it here on the street, meeting the people with no social workers, community leaders or anybody else to get in my way. I stood near the prison gates. There's security cameras outside that allow the prison staff to see people approaching. The steel prison gates open noisily when visitors are being let out, giving me a few moments to put away the crossword, pick up my tape-recorder and microphone and get ready to make my pitch.

Two young women came out. I introduced myself and asked who it was they were in to see.

It's her boyfriend so it is but he's only in for a few days for a fine.

Why would he not pay the fine?

Because he just hadn't got the money to pay the fine. He's unemployed as most people are here anyway so he just hadn't got the money to pay it. He owed a £340 fine for no road tax so he did so all he does is five days, so you're better off just going in and doing it.

Can I ask you one other thing, after the bomb at Canary

Wharf last week, do you think peace is finished now in Northern Ireland?

Well, I wouldn't like it to be finished. I have a brother in the Kesh doing twenty-two years. He's done two years. With the ceasefire being broke at the minute nobody knows how things are going to go. If the ceasefire had've lasted he would have been out a few years earlier.

Do you ever go and visit him?

All the time. The Kesh is far better conditions than what the Crumlin Road jail is.

In what sense?

It's far better. You've more privacy. You're in your own wee cubicle and you get longer time seeing the prisoners. You don't wait as long to go through which is far better. They're not allowed to smoke with the visitors in the Crumlin Road. In the Kesh they can do what they want. They have no lock up. They can sit and watch TV and videos all day if they want.

Why is it that your brother who is doing time in Long Kesh, they call it the Maze now, why do you think that people who commit politically-related crimes are treated better than the people who don't pay fines?

Well, I can't answer that.

Is your brother a loyalist or republican?

Republican.

So you think he could do a long time yet?

As it stands now he could do eighteen years whereas if the ceasefire had've upheld he would have been out in maybe eleven. You have to feel sorry not just for republican prisoners but loyalist prisoners too. They were expecting to get out a bit sooner with the ceasefire but that won't happen now.

I thanked her and we said goodbye. Why do politicals get

treated better than non-politicals? She couldn't answer that question. Neither can I.

I was glad there were no more politicals left in Crumlin Road. I find the politicals boring. They go on about things like conditions in the prison, the need for the authorities to do various things and meet various demands because that's the reality of the situation. They speak according to a formula. They never say anything interesting and they're always in the media saying it. I was here to hear other stories, other voices.

A young woman came out. She had close-cropped fair hair, heavy boots and a denim jacket and jeans. She was butch. She was friendly and keen to talk. She spoke in a rapid-fire manner, and she would throw her head or punch the air for emphasis. Her accent sounded, to me, to be as much Scottish as Northern Irish even though, she told me, she never lived in Scotland. She was from Coleraine, which she had come from that morning to visit the prison.

It's the police caused all the trouble for my boyfriend. Why don't the police let the young people alone? We were all together, Catholics and Protestants, and the police raided the rave party. My boyfriend was charged with possession with intent to supply. He's Catholic and I'm Protestant and my parents don't like him. But I'm not biased cos my husband was a Protestant, a good Orange boy like my mum and dad wanted me to marry, but they didn't care that he was beating the shite out of me in the house. (Her accent sounded even more Scottish here, complete with glottal stops. Beatin' the shi'e ou' o' me.) All I had to do was go for a drink with my friends and he used to beat me up when I got home.

Two young fellows came out. They knew me. Remember you done an interview with us before at the brew at

Corporation Street? They had just been in now to see their mate. He was on remand for fighting.

I remembered them. They were two young men who got to know each other in a juvenile prison. One was Catholic, one Protestant. We wore Celtic taps and Rangers taps, they told me, and everyone got on. (That was Celtic tops and Rangers tops, that is, football jerseys, I eventually understood when I got past their Northern vowel sounds.)

Theirs was a familiar story. Many times I have seen the sectarian divide crossed by young criminals in this way. They first get to know the other side when they get sent to prison. It was refreshing to talk to these lads. The politicals, with their insistence on segregation by religion, just leave me depressed.

A young woman described her visit.

You sit down round a table. There's about fifty people in there. You can't really talk cos everybody's so close together. You get a cup of tea, you're not even allowed a cigarette and there's people sort of looking at you.

I noticed that, the way she described it, there was no screen between her and the man she was visiting. They sat around a table and had a cup of tea. That's a more relaxed regime than in Mountjoy in Dublin. There's no heroin in Belfast so there's no need for Mountjoy-style screen visits here in Crumlin Road. Also, because the politicals were all gone from here, there was, I expect, less danger of arms or explosives going in than there used to be.

How is he?

Well he's very shaky, scared . . . he is just really pipped off.

Do you want to say the kind of thing he's accused of?

Well, it's my daddy. He's an alcoholic and he sort of beat my mummy about so he's put in there for assault, and he broke an exclusion order and things like that. (Her words mummy and daddy, in her Belfast voice, had strong and long emphasis on the first syllable. M*aaw*my and d*aa*dy.)

Was your mum right to get the order excluding him?

Oh yes, but he is still my daddy and I hate to see him in there.

Is he sorry for what he did?

Oh yes he's very sorry and at the minute he's trying to get help. We're trying to get him out of there and into a wee help centre.

May I ask you about the peace in Northern Ireland, such as it has been, do you think it will last or is it gone now, after Canary Wharf?

I think it's gone. I feel sad really because everybody has to look round you now. I mean you're really scared of a bomb no matter where you go. During the ceasefire you were able to go into town and go into parts of Belfast you never went before. Like I was in Forthriver and I never was there before in my life. But that's all over now. It's back to the same old thing, but then, what did the British government expect? They did nothing to make the ceasefire last.

In her last couple of sentences she made it clear to me that she was a Catholic, but up until then, her feelings about the ceasefire were the same that I had been getting over the last eighteen months from Catholics and Protestants alike in Northern Ireland. People deeply appreciated the ceasefire. The killings had almost stopped. You could get around and not be worried. There was no security checkpoints or searching of baggage whenever you went into a shop. In the south, I used to hear pundits saying that the nationalist people of Northern Ireland had got nothing out of the ceasefire. I thought that was a stupid observation. Everybody benefited from the ceasefire. During the ceasefire, for the first time in their lives in some cases, people had the freedom to live their lives in conditions that were close to normality.

Dark clouds were coming in over Divis Mountain. It began to rain heavily. I crossed the road and squeezed myself up against the wall of Crumlin Road courthouse. A small car pulled up and the driver, a smartly-dressed woman in her late thirties, rolled down the window. You might as well come in from the rain, she said.

I climbed in and thanked her. Who are you working for, she said? I told her it was RTE. That's what I thought, she said. When I saw you interviewing people, and wearing that hat, I guessed that you were the fellow who's on RTE on a Saturday morning. I often listen to you.

I told her she was exactly right.

I was surprised that she knew my work. When I'm out working, I rarely meet anyone who hears me on the radio. I deal, mainly, with underclass people and underclass people don't listen to RTE. But this woman was a fan. That's a good start.

She told me she had just been visiting someone in prison. She wanted to tell me about it so I turned on my tape-recorder.

How is he today, the man you were in to see?

Agitated because of the twenty-four hour lock-up.

Is he on remand?

Yes, he's still on remand. They're bored twenty-four hours a day. He sits. He reads a lot which is good. That's it really. He just sits in the cell and reads and then when he gets out he does a little bit of exercise. He has a gym facility.

Did you find it upsetting going in there, or is it something you don't really mind?

I find it upsetting.

Can you tell me . . . ?

Well, it's my son. He's twenty-one. He comes from a good home and to think that this is where he ended up is unbelievable. But the system in Northern Ireland I find is one of, well I don't know the statistics for young people, but most young fellahs between sixteen and thirty end up in bother at one stage or other. This fellah has just happened to come to a very sad . . .

She was upset. I wondered if the crime her son was in for was something worse than the usual drink-related foolishness.

I'm going to take a guess that it was something to do with drink?

It was indeed, yes. Drink has been a constant worry because I was told first of all the company that he mixed with sort of dictated his lifestyle as well so it's unfortunate what has happened. Self-gain of course to feed the addiction, the drink, as he wasn't working.

(Self-gain is a legal term meaning robbery.)

So he was breaking into places and stuff like that?

Ahuh.

There's mothers everywhere say, where did I go wrong? Is that the kind of thing that you say to yourself?

Well you do question yourself, of course. You reflect back and you think, did I do the right things? Did I bring him up right? But at the end of the day, I think everybody's given a free will. This boy was brought up the correct way. He knew right from wrong and I have a motto in life, that if you do something wrong you have to pay for it and he knew that but he got to such an extent where the drink and drugs took control and he didn't care anymore. Then there was a family breakdown. He's the eldest boy.

I knew, now, that she was Protestant. Partly, I knew because of her sort of theological language that Protestants use, but more so, it was because she accepted that her son was guilty and that he should be punished for what he had done. Protestants accept the concepts of guilt and punishment. You can be a long time waiting outside the Crumlin Road before you find a guilty Catholic.

What do you mean by a family breakdown?

Well, I was divorced so he took that bad and him being the oldest boy he took it bad as well and he went on the rampage a bit. I couldn't control him and he had to leave the house and he moved to an unsavoury area.

Some people worry about the kind of crime you can get involved with in Northern Ireland. Young men get involved with paramilitary groups. Did you ever worry about that?

Possibly ecstasy wasn't the worse thing that could have happened to him . . .

I don't understand?

Ehmm . . . he was approached by the paramilitaries. He is totally opposed to that. Because of that he received a lot of punishment beatings . . . you will do this . . . or you will join this or else and this is what he got. He came to me and he said that he didn't want to be in this country so I sent him across to England to his dad. His dad let him down and he was left to roam the streets to make a living and he came back again. The paramilitaries approached him again, he got into trouble and he had to leave the house. He moved to Belfast and that's where this trouble began.

I take it these are loyalist paramilitaries?

Of course.

I believe you're Protestant because of a couple of things you said.

I'm not biased at all. This is the situation that I find horrendous because my son was never brought up, you're a Protestant, you're a Catholic. Everybody has a right to live, everybody has their own way of going. They were taught respect.

So the loyalist paramilitaries approached him and said, you're going to work for us or we beat you up, is that how it's done?

Absolutely. That's basically how these young fellahs are forced into it. Literally forced into it.

And did he get involved?

Yes he did. He hadn't got a choice really because, in actual fact, I recall a time when they asked him to do a job, as they classed it, which was involved in drugs. This is the sickening part about it. They have their anti-drugs campaign but they're pushing drugs to raise money for their own purposes and on this occasion, my son said no. Two men approached my door with guns – I wasn't in at the time – and ordered my son out of the house, took him somewhere in a car blindfolded, beat him up very badly. I had to take him to the hospital and he was in overnight. The hospital said he could go home the next day. The paramilitaries approached him again and he brought a tin into the house, you know a tin about six inches into the house, with drugs in it which he had to do a delivery on in the middle of the night. The following day he did what he was told because he was so badly beat up, the poor fellah, and he said mummy, I can't stand this any longer. I have to leave the country. So I took him down to Dublin the next day and he took the ferry to Wales, proceeded then to get into trouble and come back, got into more trouble, ended up in a bad assault situation. He assaulted somebody. He was arrested and the judge let him out on bail. He couldn't be bailed to my home because the assault was within a mile radius of where I live so they had to get him a hostel which was on the Antrim Road. It's not a very nice place especially for young fellahs. It's very down and out, so he got into bad company on both sides, Catholic and Protestants, and this is where the big incident happened.

What was the big incident?

The incident was where my son and another boy went out one night with . . . not intentions to go out and deliberately rob somebody but the other boy was apparently quite high on drugs. My son was too and they discovered they had nothing left so they decided to go and rob somebody to the extent that they gave him a hiding. The other boy involved was the main one to that extent of the injuries the man died. So of course my son and this other chap was arrested on the grounds of murder and taken to Castlereagh holding centre which is for paramilitaries. He should not have been there. He should have gone to the Antrim Road detention centre, holding centre, because it was non-sectarian. They were classing it as a sectarian murder. In fact it wasn't. It was what they call self-gain.

The victim was a Catholic?

The victim was a Catholic.

It must wound you very badly, what has happened?

Yes, it does absolutely. It is like a death.

You're from outside Belfast. Did it affect you with your Catholic neighbours when your son got involved?

Not in the least, definitely not, very supportive so they were, very caring, very helpful. Some of my dearest and closest friends. Religion is never discussed, to be honest with you.

She gave me her address.

She told me she was aged thirty-nine. My age, too, but she had a son aged twenty-one. Yes, she said, she married young. It hadn't worked out. She was laughing as she talked about this. She seemed relaxed now. Not crying any more.

We said goodbye. It was an interview that I had expected

105

to be about her son being locked up because of drink and drugs. It turned out to be about something much worse. The big incident, she called it. Her son had kicked a man to death.

I had heard a lot of special pleading by a mother for her son. It was the drink. It was the drugs. It was bad company. His dad was no good. He was forced to do it. That's normal. I couldn't blame her for looking for excuses. I suppose any mother would. But she accepted her son's guilt. She reminded me of an older woman I met here three years before who, like this woman, was in visiting her son who had attacked a Catholic. In the case of that older woman's son, the victim had survived. Both women used the same expression to describe their feelings about what their sons had done. It was like a death.

In 1997, the year after that interview, the murder charge against that woman's son was changed to manslaughter. He was convicted and sentenced to seven years in prison. The other man who was involved in the killing was convicted of murder and sentenced to life in prison.

Mountjoy Prison, Dublin;
May 1996

A twenty-year-old woman hanged herself in Mountjoy just a few hours after she was sent there. Her name hadn't been released yet so I was going to have to be careful how I did the report. I was standing outside the prison gate. That's a good place to learn things.

The women's prison is near the main prison. It shares the same building as St Patrick's, the juvenile prison. There were a lot of social workers and other professional women in and out of the prison. I didn't want to talk to them. You can usually tell, by the look of them, which women are criminals or their visitors and which women are prison staff or other professionals.

Two young women came out who looked like criminals. I approached them and told them who I was and that I wanted to find out about the girl who hanged herself. One of the women was aged about twenty and an obvious junkie, skinny and pale with a strong Dublin accent. The other woman was about mid-twenties. She was a traveller. Big, rough and healthy-looking with a traveller's style of speech. The female prison population in Mountjoy is made up almost entirely of junkies and travellers.

The skinny woman, I can't remember her name so I'll call her Mary, told me that she didn't know Carol-Anne, the dead woman, and that none of the other prisoners knew her either. She was new to the prison and drugs scene. They heard about her death at breakfast that morning. Carol-Anne was caught shop-lifting. It was her first time in prison, said Mary. She must have had no one to talk to when she was in her cell. She shouldn't have been left alone because that's when you feel the worst. My cousin hanged herself in prison, too.

I knew the woman Mary was talking about. I said that I had stood at this very spot six years before when Sharon Gregg hanged herself in prison. I interviewed some of her fellow-prisoners that day for the *Pat Kenny Show* on radio. One of Sharon's cell-mates, Kathleen, a traveller from Dundalk, described Sharon as a good prisoner. She'd always try to cheer you up and she'd always share her fags with you. I got that obituary to Sharon Gregg broadcast on radio.

Mary was pleased that I remembered her cousin. She knew Kathleen, too. I was able to tell Mary that I had met and interviewed Kathleen since outside the Magistrates' Court in

Manchester. Kathleen was up for what she called a street robbery, but wouldn't explain to me exactly what that meant. Kathleen guessed, correctly, that because she had a baby, she wouldn't be sent to prison.

Mary wanted to talk more about her cousin. She took an old photograph out of her pocket. It was of herself and Sharon visiting Santa Claus in Dun Laoghaire shopping centre. In the photograph, Sharon was aged about fifteen and was holding the hand of her cousin Mary who was aged about eight. I pray to Sharon sometimes when I'm in my cell, said Mary.

The traveller with Mary, Maria was her name, was cautious to begin with but after a while she began to speak to me, too. She was matter-of-fact about Carol-Anne's death. Sure if they're going to hang themselves there's nothing anyone can do about it. She couldn't take the pressure, I suppose. Sure she wasn't even sentenced. She mightn't have been sent to prison at all. She mustn't have been used to it.

I think Maria had it right. Carol-Anne, I would learn over the next few days, was of middle-class background from Swords but after she became a heroin addict she moved into a flat in the inner city. It's a pattern for middle-class kids who become junkies to change their friends and their social environment and even their accent. But Carol-Anne, I guess, despite taking on the junkie lifestyle, didn't have the toughness and indifference towards the law of an inner-city person when it came to being arrested. Other young drug addicts would shrug their shoulders at a shop-lifting charge and a few hours in a cell. Carol-Anne must have found the experience overwhelming.

Did you ever feel suicidal in prison, Maria?

Maria laughed. Not any more she said. Sure I've only another two years to go.

Maria explained that she was living in Knocknaheeny in Cork. She gets the train to Dublin once a week to sign on at Mountjoy. She goes to the community welfare officer at Gurranabraher in Cork to get her return tickets. Last night she stayed chatting awhile in the prison and decided that she would stay overnight and get the train back today. When I asked why she couldn't sign on in Cork Prison or at a Cork garda station which, I thought, would save the Southern Health Board the weekly cost of the train tickets, Maria explained that she wouldn't be allowed to do that. I'm doing my sentence in Mountjoy, she said. (The Department of Justice confirmed all of this to me later. Maria has to sign on in Mountjoy because there is no women's prison in Cork.)

What were you in for, Maria?

Robbery. Handbags and all.

Did you have many friends in prison?

Most people were all right. Sometimes, when you're in the prison yard, the lads can see us out from their cells and they calls us knackers and all but most people were all right.

Maria needed to go for her train. I told them I would give them both a lift and they agreed to stay talking with me for another while.

Mary, did you ever feel suicidal in prison?

Mary answered that sometimes, when you think of all the hardship you have caused to your family through drugs, you can feel very down and wish you weren't alive any more. Alone in your cell is the worst part. But then we have great fun with the lads in St Patrick's.

How so?

The two women were smiling. Tell him, Mary, about the crack we have with the lads.

Mary laughed. Ah, yeah. You'd do anything for the buzz.

Mary described some kind of ventilation pipes that run between the floors of the prison, allowing cells to communicate with each other. The women prisoners are on the lower floors, the young male offenders are on the upper ones. And sometimes the communication is more than just words.

Well, the boys send us cigarettes. They tie them up on a string and lower them out the window and then we tie our knickers on and send them up to the boys.

This sounded familiar. I had read about this knickers-for-cigarettes swapping in the late Pat Tierney's book, *The Moon on My Back*. Pat was sent to St Patrick's in 1972, when he was fifteen. Pat looked out the window of his cell, across the prison yard to the cells opposite his, and was puzzled to see little packages being lowered on a string from the upper windows to the lower ones, then being taken in through the bars and finally raised back up again. Even when the other boys explained to Pat that the women were loaning their knickers to the boys, Pat still didn't understand. He knew nothing about wanking when he was first sent to St Patrick's.

Now, twenty-four years later, Mary was describing the same thing still going on. Sometimes the boys give us cigarettes, said Mary, and sometimes we do it just for the buzz.

We went to my car and headed for Heuston Station. We dropped Maria there and then I gave Mary a lift to the Dart station at Westland Row. She talked some more about Sharon.

Her cousin changed her mind about suicide after the noose tightened on her neck, said Mary. She had clawed at her neck with her fingernails. I dream about her still and in my dreams I save her before it's too late. She should never have been left alone.

I'm sure Mary was right. Being in the cell, alone with your despair, must be the worst part. That's when the risk of suicide is greatest.

I think about Pat Tierney whose book made such an impression on me. Pat was thirty-nine when he finally hanged himself before Aids could finish him off, but twenty-four years earlier, when he was sent to St Patrick's, it's a fair guess that he was, even then, at high risk of committing suicide. But he was helped by his friends and by the women of Mountjoy. Perhaps that help is what saved him.

So sending a young lad a warm, woman-scented pair of knickers to entertain himself with is a small act of kindness that the good women of Mountjoy have engaged in now for generations. Long may their kindness continue.

Limerick Prison;
December 1996

She was an exceptionally good-looking woman. About twenty-two, blonde, with beautiful, fine features. She had the look of a 1960s film-star. The sort of woman you would expect to see sitting in a rich man's sports car or sunbathing on his yacht. A Susan George look-alike.

She had just come out of Limerick Prison where she had been visiting her boyfriend. She was a cheeky, talkative sort of person with a mischievous smile. Of course she'd talk for the radio. She had a local accent. What do you want to know?

Her boyfriend had another eighteen months to go on a two-year sentence. He had stabbed and injured a man and later he had assaulted an arresting garda. You can get six months for common assault, she said, and anything up to two years for grievous bodily harm. He was depressed today because he had been turned down for Christmas parole. Recently he had cut his wrists and got twenty-seven stitches.

Was he drunk when he stabbed the man?

Yeah, they were well-intoxicated. (She was laughing here.) He's always in trouble through drink. Last time he was in 'twas for two common assault charges. That was drink, too.

How do you feel about his drinking?

Well, the two of us were on the warpath with one another and he went out and got drunk, but sure, men, they blame everyone but themselves. He tried to say it was my fault what he did.

Do you miss him?

I miss him terrible now over Christmas. This is the first time he's been in prison over Christmas.

How many prison sentences has he done?

Ehmmm . . . three now. The first time he done a nine month sentence for malicious damage. He smashed the windows in some cars.

This story was typical of the ones I heard all day from Limerick Prison. Whereas Mountjoy is full of Dublin junkies who are in for stealing to feed their habit, Limerick Prison is full of young culchies who do stupid or violent things when they are mad with drink.

I tried to put myself in the position of this woman's boyfriend in prison. How did he feel as he watched her walk out of the visitor's area? She was beautiful and would turn the head of any man. He must long for her. I remember one hot, summer's day interviewing women who were visiting their boyfriends in Mountjoy. They wore short skirts and gaping blouses tied up around their middles, showing off their legs, bellies and breasts. I'm sure they left their boyfriends feeling horny and frustrated with nothing else to do only go back to their cell and play with themselves. At least this Limerick woman was visiting her boyfriend in winter time and she was well-dressed against the cold. There was a question I had to ask her.

You're a very beautiful woman, does your boyfriend ever worry that other men might want you?

All the time. He never stops. Where were you and who were you with? He's just after asking me now to marry him. (She was laughing again.)

And what did you say?

I told him I'd think about it. But we can't afford to get married. It's just he's paranoid about me meeting somebody else.

And have you ever met anyone else?

Well, you can't expect me to do two years by myself, can you? But he don't know that. I tell him whatever he wants to hear. Don't worry about it, love, you'll be all right. What he don't know won't hurt him.

I had to struggle with my conscience after this one. I had a vision of the prisoner hearing his girlfriend on the radio and maybe slitting his wrists again or hanging himself. But it was an interview that I decided was too good not to broadcast. Hopefully, the fellow wouldn't have a radio on in his cell. And even if he did hear the programme, perhaps it would have a good effect on him. He might ask himself what he was doing, ruining his life with drink, when he could be with that beautiful woman instead.

There were lots of travellers visiting the prison. One of them, a young woman, agreed to talk to me.

My husband's in doing seven year. He gets his moods like, bad moods. And you can't explain to the children where he is. They're too small like. We were in England. We shouldn't have come back. He was a young boy when it happened like but when we came back he got seven year for grievous bodily harm. There's a lot of places sell him drink and they shouldn't cos he gets in trouble when he has drink. He's quietened down now, like, since he met me. I don't drink.

Did you know about this incident from his past?

I did. Like, I knew the family of the boy it happened to. They're my cousins. We shouldn't have come back from London, like, but he was lonesome and he had to come.

Seven years is a long time to wait. You're a young woman. Is it possible that you'll meet someone else?

Not if God is looking down on me, I won't. I'm married to him and I have no authority to take on anyone else. There's girls in Limerick take on again after their husbands is in prison but I'm a traveller and the travelling community don't believe in that.

She was a typical traveller woman. Self-sacrificing and loyal to her husband. She put me in mind of the traveller women I interviewed in Mitchell's Estate in Tralee a couple of years before. They were three sisters, they told me, two of whom were deserted and one widowed. They were all young women but none of them would "take on" again, not even the widow. You're only married once. You can't have your children growing up confused cos that's dirt. One of the women was nearly blind in one eye from the injury her husband, "a countryman" (a non-traveller), had given her. But she would remain faithful to her marriage vows even though he was long gone.

I say that those Tralee women told me they were sisters but now I'm not sure if they were. I described them as three sisters when I wrote about them in my last book. More recently, I visited them again in Tralee. The one I met laughed when I asked after her sisters. We're not sisters, she said. I was puzzled by this. How did I get it into my head that they were sisters? How did I make that mistake? Then, one day, I listened back to the tape of the interview with the three women as I was preparing to use it in a talk I was giving to a women's group in Tallaght. There it was at the beginning of the interview. We're three sisters. Travellers often lie to non-travellers such as myself for no obvious reason. It seems to be part of an overall traveller policy of keeping the rest of us confused and guessing.

There are IRA prisoners in Limerick. The IRA wives and supporters are an identifiable group. They often have northern accents but even before they speak, you can usually tell them by the look of them. Most prisoners and prison visitors come from the poorest parts of Ireland's towns and cities. Limerick's prisoners nearly all come from one or other of the city's two welfare ghettoes, Southill and Moyross. The wives and mothers have the look of poverty about them. They wear sneakers and track-suit bottoms. Often they wear no stockings. They have rough faces and a demeanor that comes from generations of poverty. Poor people have a look about them which is hard to describe and impossible to define, but possible to recognise nonetheless.

The IRA visitors don't look like poor, underclass people. Probably most of them are of working-class background but they are not the sort of people who end up in prison for drinking, fighting and smashing the windows of cars. In the North, IRA men smash the kneecaps of the sort of young people who end up in Limerick Prison.

Chapter Five

THE PERVERTS OF KILKENNY

South Eastern Health Board Office,
Kilkenny;
March 1995

She was a smiling, friendly woman aged about thirty. Her accent was strongly rural and she spoke with a slight lisp.

I collect a pass for to go to Dublin and see my husband. They're very good here. Once a month I get a pass here.

That's a pass for the train, yes? And you get it here from the health board Office?

Yeah. I go to see my husband once a fortnight. He's up in Dublin in prison for a rape charge.

Her cheerful tone never changed when she mentioned the crime. She might have been describing her husband being done for a parking offence.

Has your husband been convicted?

Oh, he's four years away now. He has another five to do.

It's important to you that you see him a lot?

Oh yeah. As far as the kids are concerned, I mean the kids are entitled to see him. And we still have a great relationship, I mean, there's no point letting something like that go if you can save it. D'you know?

Are you looking forward to when he gets out?

Very much so.

Is it Arbour Hill he's in? (Arbour Hill is the usual prison for sex offenders.)

That's it exactly.

How do you find the visiting in that prison?

Very nice. I've been in Mountjoy to see a brother of mine and Arbour Hill is much nicer.

Rapists can be despised. Do you find that people . . . ?

No, no. We haven't had any problems. Not where I'm living or not around the town either. You know, no one has ever said anything bad. I've great friends, you know? And everyone in my family's very good.

And how do you feel about what he did?

Well, it's not my place to judge him. I mean I can't judge. I don't have the authority to judge him.

But does it not hurt you what he did?

Well, I was able to forgive him. That's the thing. And I think if you can do that . . . I mean it was hard to begin with but if you can forgive . . . that's the thing.

The victim, does she live here in Kilkenny?

No, she's from . . . well, she was in Kilkenny but she's not from Ireland. I think she's gone back to her own place at this stage.

It must have hurt you in the beginning?

Well, it did a lot, but I got counselling and that was good. It helped me through it. He's getting counselling too in prison and I want him to keep it up.

I thanked my interviewee and said goodbye to her. It was an unsatisfactory interview but I felt I wasn't going to get any further with her than I already had. She was at once totally up front and almost completely impenetrable. She told me, with almost no prompting, that her husband was in prison for rape. But then she answered all my further questions with glib talk about forgiveness and not having the authority to judge someone. Her attitude to the victim was dismissive. She's not from here and doesn't live here any more.

I felt disturbed by the interview. I still do as I listen back to the tape to write this. It was wrong that she was so happy. She seemed to have faced up to her husband's crime by refusing to face up to the seriousness of what he had done. If this is the effect of counselling then I think that's a bad effect. I would prefer if she was still appalled at what her husband had done. I wanted her to tell me that he was never going to sleep in her bed again. Or something like that.

I'm annoyed at myself, too, that I didn't break through her defences. I tried all my usual techniques. So as to keep her talking, I never showed my disapproval of her attitude. I asked her easy questions about visiting and the like so as to build up her confidence. But when I moved in for the kill and asked about what it was like to be married to a rapist, I failed to get through. Perhaps I should have challenged her when she said she couldn't judge someone else. Why not? Why can she not judge a rapist? I wish I had a chance to do the interview again and maybe do a better job.

Later that evening in a pub in Kilkenny I learned a bit more about that rape case. The victim was a young European woman who was studying here in Kilkenny. She left Ireland after she was raped. The Kilkenny natives I spoke to in that pub didn't share my interviewee's joy at the prospect of the rapist being back among them again before too long. They wouldn't be hanging out bunting for him.

I still wonder if my interviewee that day was always prone to delusions or whether this was the effect of counselling. She and her rapist husband would not be welcome back in Kilkenny. I don't know if he is out of Arbour Hill by now but if he is, my guess is that he and his wife have gone to live in England in the anonymity of some big city. Irish sex offenders generally go to England when they get out of prison.

Arbour Hill Prison, Dublin;
June 1995

You know Arbour Hill is different from other prisons as soon as you go in. It's quiet. This was the third prison I was teaching in within one week. I had already been in Mountjoy and Wheatfield. They're noisy places where the corridors echo with the rough banter of young men with working-class accents. But Arbour Hill is different. Sex offenders include men from all age groups and from all walks of life.

I was in Arbour Hill to speak to a group of prisoners studying sociology. I knew they were going to be all, or nearly all, sex offenders, but the teacher who was in charge of the course told me he wouldn't be able to tell me the names of the prisoners or discuss what they were in for. That teacher had invited me to talk to this group about my radio work. Prisoners are usually good radio listeners and the teacher told me they were looking forward to meeting me.

A young woman teacher led me along a corridor. I was thinking that Arbour Hill is in good nick. Better than Mountjoy. Then we passed the toilets. Fortunately, there was nobody in there when we walked by. The whole washroom area is surrounded by walls the upper half of which are made of clear perspex. Likewise the toilet cubicles. A passing prison officer is able, at a glance, to see all activity in the washroom area. Prisons are always awful places, no matter how modern or well-kept they might be.

I had my notes and a few tapes in hand. I had brought a

tape of my interview of a few months before with the rapist's wife in Kilkenny. My brief was to talk about radio, rather than sex offences, but I felt that I might get to play this tape. We reached the room. There was a group of about twenty men there ranging from young to middle-aged. So these are the perverts.

They look ordinary. They don't look like criminals. I can usually tell a criminal by looking at him. If you go to your local district court you'll see what I mean. When you see two men handcuffed to each other, you can always tell which one is the cop and which one is the prisoner even if the cop is a scruffy plainclothesman. The prisoner is a scrawny young man with tattoos who speaks with an urban, working-class accent. The cop is a big culchie. You can also tell by the face and the ears. There is such a thing, I believe, as poor, working-class features and these are usually the features of criminals. But looking around me now at a room full of sex offenders, I knew that you couldn't tell a rapist to look at him. I couldn't anyway.

I recognized one man. Former neighbours had told me to expect to see him there. He was a man of about forty and I knew him slightly from the time we used to drink in the same pub in the Kimmage area of Dublin. He was a medical orderly who, over a long period, molested a young spastic woman who was in his care. Other hospital staff realised the woman was distressed and losing weight but, for a long time, they couldn't figure out what the cause was. It took several months before the victim succeeded in letting the concerned staff know what was happening to her.

I went immediately to speak to the spastic-molester and I passed on the greetings of some of his old drinking buddies. He was pleased to meet me. He looked a small, pathetic man. I knew a lot about him from other, older people in Kimmage.

121

I don't think sex offenders always come from abused backgrounds, but they often do. The spastic-molester was hated by his mum and dad because he was the product of a brief, adulterous fling on his mother's part. As a little boy, he was subjected to cruel and unusual punishments that the neighbours knew about. The neighbours remember the child's cries of terror. I suppose these days the parents would be reported but back in the 1950s and 1960s, different values obtained.

The teacher introduced me to the class. I spoke about my radio work and played a tape I had made about money-lending in Cork. It involved a couple rowing with each other about money, and lots of other things too.

What did you think of that, men?

Two fat, middle-aged men with glasses and red faces were sitting close to me on my right. They had rural accents. Totally irresponsible broadcasting, they said. Exploitation of vulnerable, uneducated people. You're using these people for entertainment.

A man behind them was raising ironic eyebrows as the two fat men were speaking. He interrupted. He had a Dublin accent. That's the reality, he said. That's what it's like for families on the dole. What would you two know about it?

I was curious about my two protagonists. I would find out a bit more about them before the day was over.

A young, surly-looking man spoke next. He wore a sleeveless jacket showing off colourful, professional tattoos on his well-developed arms. I guessed that he did body-building in the prison gym. He would be a formidable fighter. His tone was unfriendly as he challenged me. Do you ever do any good with your radio work? I mean, do you ever do anything on the courts and the police? Like I'm in for raping a woman in a caravan in Kildare cos she said it was rape and the cops and the courts took her word.

A middle-aged man with a west of Ireland accent jumped up from his chair. It's the wives are to blame. I'm just a farmer, always did my job and my wife didn't stand by me.

Shut up, said the Kildare caravan man. We're fed up listening to you. You're only here a month and it's the same bloody thing about your wife since you got here.

A small, bearded man of about fifty was smiling. He spoke with an English, West Country accent. What I want to say is that when you meet them they're wearing make-up, drinking vodka and smoking cigarettes and when they're in court they're in pigtails and wearing their school uniform. (I noticed that the Dubliner had his eyebrows raised again for me to see as the Englishman spoke.)

I answered the Englishman. I said I was surprised that his legal team had allowed the alleged victim to dress as a schoolgirl in front of the jury if his defense was that he didn't know she was underage.

The course supervisor interrupted here. Come on, men, he said. This isn't meant to be about how unfair the courts are. Paddy is here to talk about his radio work.

I decided to play the tape I had made in Kilkenny a few months before. The men heard the voice of the woman who made fortnightly visits to the prison. The Englishman and another man started smiling. When the tape finished they told me they knew that woman and knew her husband. He wasn't in the room today. He used to do counselling and classes and all that but had given it up now. We're both from Kilkenny, said the two men. I said to the Englishman that he didn't sound like he was from Kilkenny. No, he said. He was from Devon but he had lived in Kilkenny a long time.

The west of Ireland farmer was on his feet again. There

were tears in his eyes. She's a good woman. Not like my wife. My wife never comes near me.

Shut fucking up, said the Kildare caravan man.

A bald, bearded man spoke next. He had a well-educated Cork voice and the tone of a man bringing a meeting to order. I would like to see something constructive coming out of today. I would like Paddy to realise that we're not all animals or sex beasts like the media calls us. The Irish media used to have higher standards but now it's sunk to the level of the English gutter press. I hope you can see now, Paddy, that we're human beings and you can tell that to your colleagues in the media. You can't say now, Paddy, that we haven't treated you well today.

I was put on the spot. I have certainly been treated very well here today, men, thank you.

I didn't add that my meeting with them today put me in no position to judge to what degree I was speaking to beasts or animals or whatever. Being polite didn't absolve them of their crimes. As the Corkman spoke I wondered, idly, why it is that pompous Cork voices annoy me more than pompous voices in any other accent. Also, why do middle-class Corkmen always sound like homosexuals? I have had to explain this to people who are visiting Cork for the first time. The fellow you have just met isn't queer. All middle-class Corkmen talk like that.

The Kildare caravan man got back on to his being innocent. His muscles frightened me. I thought about what it must have been like for his victim. He would have been able to hold her down without much trouble. A young Dublin man said he was extradited from Liverpool because of a girl he didn't realise was underage. The farmer was on his feet again going on about his wife.

Are there any guilty men here today?

The Dublin man, he of the ironic eyebrows, spoke calmly. I'm guilty, he said. I raped a woman. I had a good job as a barman. I had a good upbringing. No excuses. I raped her. I have the most of my sentence done. I'll be out, I hope, next year.

I asked the Dublin barman if he thought that non-custodial sentences should ever be applied in rape cases, as had happened, controversially, in a recent case in Kilkenny. It's not a question I would have asked of any other man in the room because no other man accepted his guilt. But the barman's guilt was established, so I thought it was fair enough to discuss his sentence. The barman replied that a non-custodial sentence might be right in certain circumstances but that, in his own case, there were no excuses so he deserved the nine years he got.

I wondered if this Dublin barman ever got counselling in prison. If he did, then I think it did him some good. He accepted his guilt and I think was therefore better able to survive his sentence, unlike the other men who were still chewed up with anger over being found guilty in the first place. Or maybe the barman never got counselling. Maybe he had reached a certain calm through suffering interminable hours locked up in his own company. I don't know the answer, but I knew then that the barman was a man I wanted to talk to some day when he got out of prison. If he reads this now, I am asking him to please contact me.

At the end of the hour the supervisor called the proceedings to an end. The men gave me a clap. They seemed to have enjoyed the session. I suppose anything different breaks the monotony of prison. As I was tidying my tapes and notes a young man who had said nothing for the hour came up and spoke to me. He had a nervous voice. Tell them, Paddy, that we're not all animals in here. Like Father

Peter said, we're not beasts. We do a lot of good work. Those Braille books for the blind, we help make them in here.

The Dublin barman approached me and thanked me for the talk. In the moments I had to speak, I asked him about the two fat men who were criticising me. What did the barman mean when he said they would know nothing about what life was like for families on the dole?

The barman answered that those two were Brother Mick and Father Frank. They're in here because of the little boys. You serious? And they were on to me about exploiting weak and vulnerable people! I said to the barman that there seemed to be a lot of religious in here. You better believe it, he said. We could get a seminary going in Arbour Hill. But the worst one here is that farmer. There was nothing safe with him. Not his sons. Not his daughters. Not the cattle. Not the granddad. No one was safe.

I realised that I knew the farmer's case. There had been a lot about it in the media a few weeks before. You wouldn't believe what this man got up to. An ordinary-looking Irish farmer. I'll say it again. You can't tell a rapist to look at one.

I wanted to ask the teacher a whole load of things about the men I had met but I knew I couldn't abuse our friendship. I have a feeling that I'm probably not supposed to be writing this now. I went into Arbour Hill as a teacher, not as a journalist. I'm sorry if I'm guilty of an abuse of trust. It's just too good a story not to tell.

Over the weeks that followed, I thought a lot about those men in Arbour Hill. Is it possible that some of them were truly innocent? It was the Englishman who was most on my mind. The victim wore her school uniform in court, he said. I wondered if he was a monk. He had a beard. I could see him in a monk's habit. Maybe sent to a monastery in

Kilkenny as a young man, lived a celibate life then one night he gets off with a woman in a pub and he genuinely thought she was of the age of consent. There were plenty of priests in Ireland riding women half their age. Maybe this fellow was just unlucky to have ended up a despised rapist in Arbour Hill. Or maybe he was guilty with no excuses. I thought about the Dublin barman who raised those ironic eyebrows for me to see as the Englishman spoke. Perhaps the Englishman was telling me a load of rubbish. I wondered if I would ever know what really happened in the Englishman's case.

As it turned out, I found out the truth before too many weeks went by. Ireland isn't just a small country. It's an intimate country. We know each other's business. I found out the truth about the Englishman one summer's day in July of 1995 when I was driving from Dublin to Connemara. Just before the Athlone by-pass, I picked up a hitch-hiker. He was a young seaman from Kilkenny. He had come ashore at Dublin that morning on leave and was headed now for his girlfriend's house in Salthill. He was in good form.

The seaman was a radio operator and a keen radio listener. He recognized my voice and knew my work well. I got to talking about the time I was in Kilkenny a few months before. The seaman knew about the rapist whose wife I had interviewed. We've had a lot of high-profile sex cases in Kilkenny, he said. And no end of priests and brothers. People in the town are talking about it at this stage. Is it something they're putting in the Nore?

I asked the seaman if he knew about an Englishman in Kilkenny, maybe a priest or monk. I described his distinctive West Country accent. Is it possible he didn't realise his victim was underage?

127

The seaman looked at me in disbelief. Do you not realise who you're talking about? He's not a priest. He's a married man with children. Everybody in Kilkenny knows that man. His is maybe the most notorious of all the Kilkenny sex cases. He's guilty. He knew very well how old his victim was. He had to know the age of his own daughter.

Chapter Six

CONNEMARA

Summer 1995

I'll tell you how I came to be living in Connemara for three months in 1995.

John Harty has an air of faded gentry about him. I think, in a previous existence, John might have been a patron of the arts. I can imagine him in the big house, standing with his friends around the piano in the drawing room, distributing his generosity and his good humour. But John isn't an aristocrat. He's a successful young businessman. John's world, the business world, is one that I would find it hard to survive in. I prefer to have RTE pay me to make radio programmes with drug addicts and criminals and the like. I know how to do that kind of work.

Deirdre knew John Harty from chatting to him in the pub, Polly Hop's, which is at a country crossroads in County Dublin somewhere between Newcastle, Lucan and Clondalkin. We liked a band called Papa Hobo and often went to hear them at Polly's. I sometimes joined Papa Hobo on stage for a song. One night, early in 1995, I think, I was playing some U2 songs when I noticed John Harty listening. He seemed to be enjoying the music. When I finished playing, John walked up to me and asked me if I would like to be a resident musician for the summer in a place he had in Connemara. The Germans would love you, he said.

John knew nearly nothing about me except that I was Deirdre's friend and that I enjoyed a pint and a laugh in Polly's, and yet here he was offering me a job. Could this fellow be for real?

That's sounds great, I said, but where will I live? John said he'd get me a house. Three bedrooms, detached. He had a share in a complex of houses called Clifden Glen. Live there and play music in the evenings, he said, as he put a pint of Guinness in one of my hands and asked me if I'd like a small one for my other hand.

A house in Connemara sounded like an answer to my prayers. Separated dads such as myself have a problem getting somewhere of our own to be with the kids. John Harty seemed too good to be true. I was told a long time ago never to believe promises made in pubs. But I shouldn't have doubted John Harty. He was as good as his word. A few weeks later, Deirdre and I took him up on his offer of the use of a house in Clifden whenever we wanted it. It was the holiday weekend of St Patrick's Day, 1995, that we began our discovery of Connemara.

The Borstal Graveyard in Letterfrack

I was never in Connemara before but I had heard of Letterfrack. Dubliners who were once young criminals told me about the place. The school at Letterfrack served as a borstal and also as an orphanage. It was in service from late in the last century until it finally closed in 1973. This was a borstal in an age before drugs when crime was rare. But kids who mitched school or stole things from shops got sent to Letterfrack. So here was this place on the west coast, surrounded by bogs and mountains, 200 miles from Dublin and yet its name was familiar to generations of working-class Dubliners and they, in turn, had made it familiar to me.

Deirdre and I found the old school building at Letterfrack easily enough. It looks like any other national school building of its day. It's a gaunt place surrounded by a schoolyard. Up behind the school, there's a row of cottages and, further up some stone steps up a steep slope, there's a church. I recognised this much of Letterfrack from Mannix Flynn's novel, *Nothing to Say*.

Flynn's novel has to be largely autobiographical. It's set in the 1960s and it's about a Dublin child sent to Letterfrack for petty theft and mitching from school. After being sentenced, the child is handcuffed to a policeman and brought by train to Galway. Then a Christian Brother collects him to bring him by car the rest of the way across the wilderness of Connemara. At Letterfrack, in those cottages behind the school, the child gets kitted out with a hairy shirt, boots and overalls. In the freezing mornings they were marched out to assemble in the schoolyard before climbing those stone steps up to the church for Mass. Then it was out to the fields and the bogs to labour for the day.

The boys were inadequately fed and inadequately clothed. They were kids from the poorest parts of Dublin and were probably always sickly and underfed. To this day, culchies are generally bigger than Dubliners and I think that difference was even greater in the past. So the poor Dublin kids didn't have a chance when the Brothers decided that the children needed to be beaten. A man in Connemara whom I got to know over the next few months of 1995 told me he had vivid memories from the 1940s of Christian Brothers kicking the children they brought with them on work parties. In Flynn's novel, the Christian Brothers don't come across as irredeemably wicked. The man who sexually assaults the boys in Flynn's account is the gardener, rather than one of the religious. The Brothers show touches of humanity and concern for the boys, but the practice of stripping and beating is routine.

It's not easy to find the borstal graveyard. Flynn makes no mention of it in his book but Deirdre and I knew it was there because we read about it in Tony Whilde's guide book to Connemara. Whilde said that this is where the little boys who died at Letterfrack are buried.

We looked near the church but found only one grave. It was the grave of a priest who served there. The children's graveyard was nowhere obvious. Eventually we found the place. I'll tell you how to find it because I think more people should visit it. You go uphill on a road to the left of the school building, past the church and youth hostel on your right, past the sign where it says "No Entry to the Connemara National Park" and before you reach the building that was once the school's hospital and is now a park office, there's a small gate on the left leading to a path through the woods. The path leads to another small gate. This one is of wrought iron and has a cross on it, the only sign there is that you're approaching what might be hallowed ground. Beyond the gate there's a clearing in the trees about the size of two houses. You can get the onion smell of wild garlic here. It's a smell you often come across in Connemara.

The clearing is divided into two plots, each one surrounded by a low, concrete kerb. It's like two large, mass graves, but there's only one headstone, a stone cross about two metres in height standing alone at the end of one plot. As we walked toward the cross to read the inscription the ground squelched under our feet. This graveyard is in a bog.

The stone cross has sixty male names around the base. The dates of death are from 1896 to 1956. The inscription reads that those buried here are remembered by the Christian Brothers and that the cross was erected in 1969. There's nothing that says that it's children who are buried here and there's no explanation as to why their grave was not marked until thirteen years after the last interment. Somebody who happened on the graveyard and who read the inscription would probably assume that the dead were members of the Brothers.

Something terrible happened here. You can feel it. And it's not just a bad feeling without explanation. There are too many things about this graveyard in Letterfrack that don't add up. Why were sixty boys buried in an unmarked grave in a bog?

In Ireland you're supposed to be always sure of a good send-off. But the kids in Letterfrack were buried without a name, in a bog, hidden away in the woods. I think that says a lot about the way they were regarded in life. They weren't thought worthy of the respect due to kids from better-off backgrounds.

I got to know one survivor of Letterfrack in Dublin in 1987. Thomas McNally, from Drimnagh, was a couple of years older than myself. Thomas died in 1991 when the heroin habit that he had kicked many years before finally caught up with him in the form of Aids. Thomas was sent to Letterfrack as a child. He wasn't an orphan, he was a criminal. Thomas told me that one of the insults that the Christian Brothers used was to call a boy a "banbh", which Thomas understood was Irish for a piglet or runt (a small, white thing would be a close, literal translation, Irish scholars tell me). Another favourite way of hurting a boy, Thomas told me, and I think this is revealing, was to insult the boy's mother.

Deirdre and I studied the names of the dead around the

headstone. Sometimes the same unusual surnames occur two or three times. I guess many of these boys were orphans. Others, no doubt, were the sons of whores or young unmarried mothers. I expect that most kids who died at Letterfrack had their bodies sent back to wherever they came from for burial. But none of the boys who were buried here had anyone to claim their bodies back. That means that they had nobody to claim them, either, when they were alive. They were sent here and forgotten by the rest of the world, left to the care of the Christian Brothers. Nobody questioned the Church in those days. The power of the Christian Brothers over these boys was absolute.

Let me tell you about Pat Tierney. Pat wrote an extraordinary book called *The Moon on my Back*. It was about his own life. The Moon was his nightmare, his past that was catching up on him in the form of the Aids virus. Pat caught Aids through heroin use in America. He published his book in 1993 and later produced a version of his story for the stage. In January of 1996, by which time he was in a late stage of the Aids virus, Pat Tierney took his own life. That was on his thirty-ninth birthday. Pat's body was found hanging from a tree in a churchyard somewhere on the northside of Dublin.

Pat was born in January of 1957. That made him my age exactly. But he went through more suffering in his early years than I have done in all my life. Pat and I were born in the same month but in very different circumstances. I was lucky. I had loving parents. Pat was not lucky. Pat's mother was a seventeen-year-old Galway girl who put him into care. She was probably forced to give him up. Pat never knew his father. Pat was sent to Daingean, an orphanage which, I guess, was much the same as Letterfrack.

Pat Tierney's account of his upbringing in care is heartbreaking. He was physically and sexually assaulted throughout his childhood. One Christian Brother molester was known as The Pixie. He was small and fat with a cow's-lick hairstyle. He liked to take the boys' pants down and play "jellies on a plate" with their buttocks. The boys preferred The Pixie to the thugs who stripped and beat them. Pat had his nose broken by one of the thugs.

Another time Pat shit his pants and was made to stand in front of the class showing off his soiled underwear. It was no wonder the poor fellow ran away from the place as soon as he could. I believe Pat was destined for a life of crime because of the crimes committed against him as a child. Pat escaped from care when he was fifteen and he was promptly arrested in Galway city for stealing. He was sent to St Patrick's Institution, the juvenile prison at Mountjoy in Dublin.

After prison, Pat Tierney set about finding his mother. He had, he explained, a childish belief that his troubled young life would all come right if he could only be with his mother again. Many times, in his mind, he rehearsed what that moment would be like when his mother would embrace him once more. He traced her to Rochester in England. He found that she had a new life of her own and didn't want to know him. After that, Pat went to America, became a drug addict, caught Aids and came back to Ireland for the last years of his life. That's when he started writing. (I know it doesn't sound it from the description I've given here, but Pat's book, as well as being tragic, is hilariously funny.)

I thought about Pat Tierney when I stood in the children's graveyard in Letterfrack. The boys buried in what was an unmarked grave in a bog can never tell their story. But Pat lived long enough to see Ireland change. The men who bullied and sexually assaulted the young Pat Tierney thought that they were untouchable. They were the Church. Pat Tierney was a poor, "illegitimate" child whose disgraced

135

mother had run to England for refuge. Who would ever take this child's word against their word? The Christian Brothers could never have imagined that Ireland would change. The day would come when the child they brutalised would have his story published and his words listened to on radio and television.

You wrote about them, Pat, and you hurt them. Well done. I think you got them back and yet, in your suicide interview in the *Sunday Tribune*, you said you were hanging yourself in a churchyard as an anti-clerical protest. I think that was a dreadful thing to do. It must have been a terrible shock for whoever found your body. Supposing children had found you? What were you thinking of? I accept that you wanted to end your own life before the full suffering and degradation of Aids took hold. I think that was your right. But there was no need to do it the way you did. You got the Church back with your book. You didn't have to hang yourself too.

More and more stories are being told these days by people who survived orphanages. In 1994 Mary Phil Drennan wrote her account of an orphanage at Rushbrooke, near Cobh. She called her book *You May Talk Now*. I was in the same class as Mary Phil Drennan. I can't place Mary Phil but I remember many of the other orphan girls whom she refers to in her book. There were three distinct groups in the classroom. There were the Catholic day pupils such as myself who occupied most of the room. There were the Dutch kids who didn't have to stand for the Angelus and whose fathers worked at Verolme Cork Dockyard. And, always clustered together at the back of the classroom, there were the orphan girls who lived at the convent with the nuns.

I felt sorry for the orphans. I thought of their lives as school without end. I went home after school. They stayed stuck with the nuns all the time. I remember that the orphans were generally slow learners and I remember, too, that some kids despised the orphans. Always a smell of piss off them, Paddy, one child used to say to me. (The same person, as an adult living in Dublin, is still as maladjusted and misanthropic as he was as a child in Cobh. I once heard him in Tallaght teaching his little boy to shout insults at the "knackers".) I didn't look down on the orphans. I understand now that, as a London child, I didn't share in the Irish class or caste values that other kids learned. I still don't.

Mary Phil Drennan's book shocked me. I knew that the orphans had it rough but I had no idea how rough. As a child from a normal background, I couldn't have imagined what the people I sat with in the classroom were going through after school hours. Mary Phil describes beatings, endless insults and, as in other orphanages, an obsession with soiled underwear.

Each girl had only one pair of knickers to last her for the week. If, at the end on the week, a girl was found to have a stain on her knickers then she had to wear them on her head for the day. Mary Phil used to secretly wash her underwear on a Thursday night and then sleep with it under her pillow so that she would have a dry and presentable pair of knickers for the Friday morning inspection.

The girls were beaten for bedwetting. As they got older, they were beaten for having their period. They were beaten if they were sick. Mary Phil describes one child who was beaten one morning because she complained about pains in different parts of her body but was unable to tell the doctor exactly where. That child died some months later. She had leukemia.

It's no wonder that the orphans were slow learners. You can hardly expect a child to be good at school work when her "home" life is filled with fear, cruel punishments and emotional trauma.

Most of the orphan girls never completed secondary school. They variously left to take jobs, to go to England or to get married young. When Mary Phil left school, she set about trying to find out where she came from. She discovered that she was of Ulster Protestant background and that her mother ran away from home and, in Mary Phil's words, worked on the quays in Cork city. Mary Phil doesn't know who her father was, although, she says in her book, she would still like to trace him if she could. It was important to Mary Phil that she should find out what she could about how she came to be brought up in an orphanage. I don't know where Mary Phil Drennan is now but if she reads this, then, as a childhood classmate, let me wish her well.

When the Goldenbridge orphanage story erupted I thought about my own experience of Rushbrooke and my childish ignorance about what was going on there. The Goldenbridge women tell stories of having suffered beatings, psychological torture and, you guessed it, an obsession bordering on mania about the condition of their underwear.

Other people have come forward to say they remember no such cruel regime at Goldenbridge. One homeless, alcoholic man I interviewed for television at the welfare office at Charles Street in Dublin told me that he was brought up in an orphanage in Rathdrum, Co Wicklow, and that the nun there, who was also in charge of Goldenbridge, was, in his words, like a mother to him. I don't doubt his word about his own experience, but I don't doubt the words of the Goldenbridge women, either. I think, perhaps, the nuns had favourites, or maybe they treated boys and girls differently.

Some outsiders, who were not orphans, declared the Goldenbridge women to be liars or at least mistaken. A politician from the Goldenbridge area went on television to say that he was once a frequent visitor to the orphanage and he saw no cruelty towards the children. I think that politician's recollections count for nothing. My memories of Rushbrooke are mainly happy ones but Mary Phil Drennan's book showed me that nobody knows what goes on behind closed doors.

In 1997, I met Christina Noble who wrote the book *Bridge Across my Sorrows*. Christina was born in 1944 and grew up in the Liberties of Dublin. She was still a child when her mother died. Her father was a violent man and an alcoholic. Christina and her brothers and sisters were eventually taken into care. Christina was sent to an orphanage at Clifden. One of her brothers, Sean, was sent to Letterfrack.

The nuns told Christina that her brother was dead when, in fact, he was living only a few miles from her. Sean nearly did die at Letterfrack, Christina now knows. What happened was that he tried to escape from Letterfrack and got soaking wet in the process. He was recaptured and made to stand in the schoolyard in his wet clothes for the rest of the day. He got pneumonia. So, Christina tells me, he nearly ended up in that grave in the bog. These days Christina works looking after street children in Vietnam and, more recently, in Mongolia. Sean, her brother, now runs a pub somewhere in Switzerland.

My old friends, Thomas McNally and Pat Tierney, both of whom I got to know in the last years of their lives; Mary Phil Drennan, Mannix Flynn, Christina Noble, all of these people went through the orphanages or borstals and were mauled by the experience. At least they came out alive. Not like the boys buried in the bog at Letterfrack.

These days I visit Connemara a lot and I go to the graveyard at Letterfrack. The wild flowers you will see on the headstone are very likely left there by me. The boys buried there were never able to tell the story of what happened to them. If their bones could talk, what stories would they tell?

But other boys survived and now Ireland is willing to listen. Over the years, the story of Letterfrack will be told.

The George Michael of Connemara

I got to know Connemara through that long, hot summer of 1995. I walked its hills and enjoyed its beauty. And I was fulfilling a teenage dream about being a full-time musician.

Most important of all, I had a house to myself and that meant that I had the chance to live with my children again after my marriage break-up the previous year. For too long I had been a McDonald's Dad. That means you're always bringing your kids to places rather than just sharing in the routine things of everyday living. Now I had a place of my own and the children loved it here. Connemara was where I ceased to be a McDonald's Dad.

I was booked to play music two nights a week in Clifden but I usually played four or more. Ah come on, Paddy, said the Germans. Please, vee haf some music tonight. Play us Viskeys in ze Jar. They were too nice to say no to and besides, they always filled me up with drink. I also had a date once a week in the Pier Bar in Cleggan after the publican there, the very glamorous Una Churchill, heard me play a few songs in Barry's in Clifden that first night I was in Connemara back on St Patrick's Day. Una booked me for the summer. Deirdre got me dates, too, in Murray's on Inisbofin. Bofin is a place I'll tell you more about later.

In Connemara, Deirdre and I got to know George. George is a tall and handsome young man with startling brown eyes.

He's a sort of younger version of George Michael, which is why I'll call him George. His hair is sometimes fair, sometimes bleached blonde. He's always changing it.

George has a camp, effeminate way of speaking. His manner is effusive and flamboyant. When I last met him I was with two women friends in a pub and George hugged and kissed all three of us. On another occasion, George worried Deirdre when she thought he said that I had a lovely arse. She mis-heard him. In fact he had said that I had lovely eyes.

George is homosexual. I liked George. Even as I write this, I'm looking at a photograph of the two of us singing together in a pub one night, both of us suntanned in what was the summer of 1995. That photograph brings back good memories.

George couldn't hide his homosexuality even if he tried. That last time I met him, the time he kissed me, I realised I had forgotten quite how camp he is. So how have you been getting on, George? George talked about romances of the past year. He can shock you without meaning to when he suddenly talks about fellows he "snogged". He did actually snog a woman during the last year. And George, did you enjoy that? George replied, I closed my eyes and imagined I was kissing Brad Pitt.

In the pub that night, there was a man just back in Connemara after a few years working in San Francisco. He was on his mandatory week on the beer. I was talking to him and he looked at one of my women friends and asked me, who's the cute blonde? George immediately turned round to the fellow and pouted.

George was a good barman. Good with people and good at sending me drinks. George is the sort of barman who can set the right atmosphere for the whole pub. The foreigners loved him. The Dutch and German and English women used to be all over him. What is it about queers that women like so much?

But George was more interested in men than in women. Once I was sitting at the bar, chatting with George, when a pair of queers came in for a drink. (Yes, their homosexuality was *that* obvious.) One had a working-class Dublin accent, the other was a Frenchman. The two of them were make-up artists. They were working on a photography project, looking after the appearance of some women who were modelling clothes, I think. The project involved using the Connemara landscape as a backdrop. The make-up artists were sharing a house, for a week, along with the models.

Pretty soon that night, the two queers were flirting with George and he with them. He was wiggling his hips as they blew kisses at him. I left. I met George again the next day. He was in a distressed state.

After the pub closed, George had gone home with one of the make-up artists (I can't remember which one) and the other one found them together behind the house and got jealous. George ended up in the house in the middle of the night trying to solve this lovers' tiff. Nothing *really* happened between them, he told the jealous one. The models were wakened by the commotion downstairs and were kept awake all night. There was a lot of crying and shouting, then making up then more crying and shouting, said George. The next morning, the models complained to the landlord about George. No amount of make-up would hide the bags under their eyes and the day's photographic session had to be called off. They told the landlord they would never stay in one of his houses again. As the landlord and the publican were in business together, George thought he was going to lose his job in the bar.

As it turned out, George didn't lose his job. The landlord took a lenient view. That said something to me about why George stayed living in his native place, rather than in Dublin or some other city. George lived for a while in Dublin but he didn't like it there. Dublin frightened him, he told me. People in Connemara liked George. People were kind to him and George needs kindness.

I think homosexual men have an above-average tendency to suffer from mental illness. I wasn't surprised when George told me he was in hospital for a while over the winter. He was suffering with depression. Just as I have seen him go "high" with his over-the-top behaviour, so, too, I can imagine him going low. The winter is the worst for him, he told me, when Connemara empties of tourists and he, very likely, ends up on the dole for months. Once, when he was at his lowest, George was upset by the advances made on him by a local married man, a secret homosexual, who came to his flat one night and offered George money in return for sex. The man seemed to think that George would sleep with just anybody.

Once George turned up at the bar with bruises on his face. What happened to you? I fell off my bicycle, he told me. I didn't believe him. I think he was beaten up. George attracts attention. He means no harm but when he loses the run of himself, kissing men and all that, incidents can happen. So some drunk who wants to find somebody to beat up will find a likely victim in George. Now that I think of it, I don't believe George even had a bicycle.

George told me and Deirdre more and more about himself as the summer went on. Life was rough on him. He went through a lot in his teenage years. He was adopted and never knew his real mother or father. His adoptive parents in Co

Galway broke up due to "Dad's" drinking. Dad lost what had been a good business and the family home was taken away by the building society.

George lived for some years with a fellow a few years older than himself who used to beat him up if he so much as talked to any other boy. He escaped that and he told me he won't make the same mistake again. Dad doesn't drink now and lives by himself in a flat and is self-employed. George is fond of the adoptive parents whom he calls Mum and Dad and keeps in contact with both of them.

George talks a lot about his real mother. It seems to me that he's being drip-fed with information by his adoptive parents. I think they probably know more than they're telling him. George knows that his mother is just seventeen years older than he is and that she is from Cork city. George also found out that his mother was a hairdresser.

George told me he wanted to meet his real mother and that his adoptive mother was doing her best to make that meeting happen. I said to George that he would have a good chance of finding his mother for himself, especially if she was willing to be found. Cork city is not that big and people from the hairdressing business know each other. Some people in the business today may remember who had a baby the year of George's birth. Maybe she's still living in Cork. Perhaps she has the same startling brown eyes as George has.

My guess is that George's adoptive mother is trying to divert him, for the while at least, from meeting his real mum. There would be risks in the meeting. Maybe George's real mum is married now with children. Perhaps her husband doesn't know about her past. She may not want to meet the son she gave up all those years ago. Maybe she will be upset to discover her son's homosexuality. Maybe George will be upset if the meeting doesn't go as he hopes it will. So perhaps George's adoptive mother has thought about the risks and is trying to shield her adopted son from what she fears might go wrong.

George has left Connemara now but still lives in Ireland. So far as I know, he hasn't yet met his mother. But I think George has already found room for her in his heart. He won't forget about her. Sooner or later, he'll come looking.

The Ghost Villages of Killary and Inisbofin

I walked the southern shore of Killary Harbour a lot. Killary is a fjord about ten miles long that divides Connemara, to the south, from Mayo, to the north. Looking across to the Mayo side, up the steep slope of Mweelrea, Connaught's highest mountain, you can see the ridges of what were potato drills, now abandoned. These were called lazy beds although how they got that name, I can't imagine. There was nothing lazy about trying to grow potatoes up a mountain with the help of seaweed and manure. No doubt, the people who once tended these slopes also lived on food from the sea-shore. (Deep-sea fishing only began about the middle of the last century when, under the stimulus of capitalist imperialism, Connemara fishermen began to use improved boats and industrially-produced nets.)

Once, while walking Killary, for no particular reason, I decided to turn inland from the path and I climbed uphill. After just a few minutes climbing, over a ridge, I came across a cluster of ruined houses. It's a lost village, not visible from the path by the shore. It's not on the ordnance survey map. I don't know what it was called although I see, from old parish maps, that the area was roughly in what was the townland of Foher. I'll call my abandoned village Foher.

There are the remains of seven stone houses in Foher. The houses were tiny. Some have one room, some two, but the rooms were barely large enough for a man to lie down in. The roofs, which I expect were thatched, are all gone, leaving just the stone walls, now mostly fallen down. The lazy beds are clearly visible all around these houses, raised up from the boggy ground in what was an attempt to keep the potato roots dry.

I spent many solitary hours in Foher, reading, resting, thinking. Nobody ever interrupted me there. Nobody ever came near me. This was my village. I don't believe in ghosts but, in my mind, I came to know the people of Foher and the way that they lived.

The Foher people may have had goats in which case they would have had milk to go with their potato and seafood diet, although I doubt that they, as poor people, would have had more than one beast per family. Maybe the animals were tethered outside these little cottages. There are feral goats on the hills today so these may be descended from the goats of Foher. In the cold nights of winter, people brought their animals in for warmth, just as people do in parts of Africa today. (I remember drinking coffee in a toucal, a simple, circular house, in rural Ethiopia. As my eyes adjusted to the gloom, I jumped with shock when I realised I was face-to-face with a huge-horned buffalo.)

I read books about the Great Irish Famine when I was in Foher; 1995 was the 150th anniversary of the Famine and a lot of books on the subject were published that year. The Great Famine devastated Connemara. Through starvation, disease and emigration, the population fell in ten years from 33,000 to just 21,000. Foher, I feel, was abandoned during the

Famine. Those lazy beds would yield only black, rotting tubers. The goats were killed and soon there was no food left. Perhaps the Foher people died, weakened with hunger, lying in the tiny rooms of their houses. Or maybe some of them made it as far as the Union in Clifden. In November 1846, a feeding sub-station was established at "the Killaries", not far from Foher. Perhaps this saved some lives.

The Foher people, and many thousands like them, died because they were poor and politically unimportant. No political party stood for their interests. The landlord class was well represented in both Britain and Ireland. The emerging tenant-right movement represented the farmers who wanted to get the best price for their produce. No political force emerged to champion the people who were starving.

Sometimes I would climb higher up the mountain as, I'm sure, the courting couples of Foher used to do. There are hollows up high where the streams have cut through the peat of the mountainside leaving the rocks exposed below. Nothing has changed here for thousands of years. I know I am seeing what the Foher people saw.

It's a strange, other world when you get up high in the wilderness. No people, just the sound of the streams and the pipits. It's not just peaceful, it's eerie. I think I understand how these high, inaccessible slopes were regarded as holy places or magical places to be feared. This spiritual quality of the landscape would not have been lost on the Foher people either. The Foher people weren't Catholics in a way that we would recognise today. They were basically pagan with a few superficial Catholic ideas stuck on. And as pagans, sex would not have been taboo for them. It was a pleasure they made the most of.

Looking some miles out to sea beyond the mouth of

Killary, you can see Inisturk and, just south of that, Inisbofin. I never got to visit Inisturk but I grew to love Inisbofin.

Like everywhere else in Connemara, the landscape of Inisbofin is marked by the past. You can tell it was once a busy place. In centuries past, the sea was the equivalent of a highway and Bofin was central to control of that highway. The harbour at Bofin was once occupied by the pirate-queen, Granuaile. After that, Cromwell's forces built a fort there that still stands today.

Inisbofin is full of abandoned houses. These aren't just tiny pre-Famine cottages such as those of Foher. The Bofin houses were better built and a bit bigger. Many still have their roofs. In the high ground of what's called the Middle Quarter of the island, there's a ghost village. It was abandoned within living memory.

At the beginning of the 20th-century, Inisbofin had about ten times its present population of around 250. It wasn't the famine that killed off Inisbofin. It died because people wanted more out of life than fishing and subsistence farming. There was a time that there was nothing better over the next hill. But industrialisation changed all that. Irish people left the limited existence of rural life to become part of the British working-class.

It's the loneliness gets to you here. And the boredom. So said an old Bofin man I met one day when I was walking the north shore of the island with my children. We often walked that shore. You're likely to see Atlantic Grey Seals coming into the inlets there. These are much bigger animals than the Common Seal that you would see in Cork Harbour or Dublin Bay or wherever. We spotted the old man collecting periwinkles. His currach, complete with outboard motor, was pulled in on the stony shore. He had the big build and weathered features that are typical of Connemara men. He was glad to meet us. Come over and talk to me.

My daughter looked into the bucket full of periwinkles. Do you eat them? Indeed I don't, he said. I sell them to the Frenchman comes to Cleggan once a week.

The man told us he was born on Bofin and left to go to England when he was sixteen after his eldest brother took over the land. He went to work in the building industry in London. Later, he became a clerk of works for Harringay Council. He had children and now grandchildren in London. Then his brother died and he came back to Bofin to take over the land.

Forty acres of bloody nothing, that's what I have here. There was bitterness in his voice. It's the loneliness gets to you here. And the boredom. Sure, what do I want minding sheep? You meet people in the summer but I can't face another winter. Five winters we spent here and this will be the last. We're moving back to London in the spring.

The old Bofin man's attitude reminded me of the attitude of old people I met one Christmas in the Irish Centre in Digbeth in Birmingham. One woman, in her eighties, told me she went back to her home town of Kinsale a few years before but she found it a sad experience because she knew nobody. She was a stranger in what was once her home town. In Birmingham she had children and grandchildren. She would live out the rest of her life in Birmingham.

I enjoyed myself playing music in Inisbofin. Once, in Murray's, I played from something like nine in the evening to maybe four the following morning. People kept asking me for songs, and I did my best to oblige. In Murray's, the crowd were generally Irish. (For some reason, the Germans don't seem to get to Bofin except as day-trippers.) And because they were Irish, a lot of people there knew my radio work. As word would filter around the pub as to who I was, I was made to feel like a celebrity. That was nice. I love being the centre of attention.

Certain songs came to mean a lot to me that summer. Phil Colclough's *Song for Ireland* always felt right. Living on your western shore, I saw summer sunsets and asked for more; stood by your Atlantic Sea, and sang a song for Ireland. Colclough, I'm told, is a Londoner who fell in love with this place. His was a song that I understood.

Sometimes I would spend the night singing Bob Dylan or the Beatles or Neil Young. You never know what mood will take you or take the crowd. Songs evoke memories. Various parts of our lives can become associated with songs and, through music, I can get in touch with other people's memories too. Tom Waits sings about that. The music plays and you display your heart for me to see. Once, in Murray's, there were old people from Wicklow there so I sang the Thomas Moore song, *The Meeting of the Waters*. I could tell from the reaction of those Wicklow people that this song was part of their lives, too.

Deirdre and I spent days walking Inisbofin together. We passed many hours on the mile-long, sandy stretch of beach on the east side of the island. From that beach, we looked back to the mainland at the gleaming quartzite peaks of the Twelve Bens and, further north, through the haze, to the white cone of Croagh Patrick in Mayo.

We made that beach a nude beach. It's such a long stretch of sand that you always had several minutes warning of anyone approaching. After a day like that, certain songs have a special meaning. I used to sing a song from the Saw Doctors. On this fine summer's evening, as the blue of night descends, never mind the strangers cos I'll always be your friend.

It was a good summer.

Chapter Seven

IN THE COMPANY OF MEN:
IRISH BUILDING WORKERS IN GERMANY

Berlin,
October 1995

The Oscar Wilde pub was jammed. Sundays are an important day for the Irishmen here in Germany. It's the builders' day off, so men working in Berlin and for maybe a hundred miles around gather here to drink. Cars and vans lined the Friedrichstrasse outside the pub. Down the road you can see the Brandenburg Gate and beyond it what was West Berlin. The Oscar is just inside what was East Berlin.

It was freakishly warm weather for October, as what had been the hot summer of 1995 still wouldn't come to an end. Men stood outside in the sunshine with their drinks. A lot of the men here have worked in England a long time. A few years before, Canary Wharf was the place to be. Now the big money was in Germany as the former East Germany was undergoing massive investment from former West Germany. Every apartment block was being re-built or upgraded. Every filthy factory or power station was being replaced. Roads were being brought up to western standards.

There were as many English accents as Irish. A young man

with a Liverpool accent asked me if I was Armagh Mick. I told him who I was and what I was doing. He explained that, at first sight, he had mistaken my small tape-recorder for a mobile phone. Armagh Mick was expected to be at the Oscar and was believed to be looking for men for a big job in Leipzig. A sub-contractor, such as Mick, can usually be spotted by his mobile phone at his hip. The Oscar, I was learning, wasn't just a place to drink. It's also a place for men to hear about and be recruited for work. The Oscar is where all the deals and the important decisions are made.

I went in and squeezed my way up to the bar. It was noisy. Sinead O'Connor was wailing over the music system. The barman, the very friendly Terry from Derry, remembered me from the last time I was in his pub in 1992. God, yes, he said, I remember the last radio programme you made here. There was a lot of trouble over that programme, Terry told me, and he, as the barman in the Oscar, had to deal with agitated phone calls from Ireland after the programme was broadcast.

What happened was this. In 1992, I interviewed a Dublin man in the Oscar who talked about the liberal attitude that German women have to sex. This Dubliner gave up lorry-driving and went into the furniture business in Berlin. He moved in with a German woman and they had a son but soon afterwards she was seeing another man. Then she left Berlin along with her child. German women are too liberal, the Dubliner laughed. Humour seemed to be his way of getting over the hurt. But it was all news to his mum and dad when they recognized their son's voice on the radio. They didn't know they were grandparents. Terry had to deal with the calls from Ireland as these grandparents tried to track down their son.

There had been trouble as well, Terry told me, over the

County Limerick woman I interviewed at the American military base. She was ten years in Berlin and was apart from her German husband. Her mum and dad never knew about the marriage break-up. Every Christmas over the last few years, she told them that Hans, or whatever his name was, couldn't make it to Ireland this time because of pressure of work. Now, since the radio programme, everybody in that woman's Limerick village, including her mum and dad, had learned the truth.

Why, Terry asked me, do people say things like that on the radio? Did they not realise what they were doing? I couldn't answer the question very well, but I said sometimes people find it easier to tell something in public rather than in private.

I remember when I was fairly new at radio work, back in 1986. A man in a snooker hall in Watercourse Road in Cork told me he had spent the electricity money on drink. My wife thinks I paid the bill, he said. And was he worried that she would hear him on the radio and learn the truth? It's time she learned the truth, he said. Likewise, a few years later, I was outside a gaming machine arcade in Limerick city. A man who walked past me at first, seemingly in an angry mood, came back a few minutes later to tell me how sick he felt after blowing all his money on a gambling machine. He had lost his job as a commercial traveller because of his gaming addiction. He spent company money that he couldn't pay back. Now he was on the dole and his wife thought he was finished gambling but he got the odd nixer that his wife didn't know about. He had just spent seventy quid on the poker machines and hated himself for it. And supposing his wife heard this on the radio? He needed to tell her, he said, and now he had found a way to do it.

I made my way around the Oscar Wilde pub and quickly

learned two things. First, almost every man here old enough to be married is separated. Second, every man here has been "knocked" by sub-contractors at least once. To be knocked is to be cheated out of your money. A job may last a few weeks. A man might get a "sub" of money after a week or so but, time and again, it happens that the sub-contractor cannot be found when the finishing money is due to be paid. There were often violent incidents over money. It pays to have a violent reputation when doing business with the Germans, I was told. But these men knew they were at a language disadvantage and that they could be deported if they got into trouble with the police. This is the Wild East. There's big money here. For working a seventy-hour week, a man expects to earn £1000 without tax, but he has no security of any sort. There are accidents with no compensation and always the danger of being knocked.

Three men at the bar were well drunk. They were knocked, they told me, and they were taking a few days off to go on the beer. No point working if you're not going to be paid. They were all married and had since separated. Their wives, all Irishwomen, were living in London. It's the lifestyle, they told me. You can't keep a marriage together if you're always away from home. And could they not get work in England? Yes, but not work that paid you well enough. They asked me to get them a drink. I said okay, but I realised that these guys must have a serious drink and money problem. Most men in the pub had been trying to buy drink for me. But these three men were different. There was a kind of menace about them when they realised I was good for a drink. I felt trouble coming. Then came Lofty.

Ah, Mr Lofty, they said. Lofty is a great laugh. Come over here, Lofty, there's a man from RTE buying drink.

Lofty was a tall man of about thirty with a Wicklow accent.

154

Buy me a drink and I'll talk to you, he said. He was aggressive and had a mad look, but the pub was so noisy that his carry-on went without being noticed by anyone else. I bought a round of drinks. Lofty snarled at me, holding up his whiskey. I'm not drinking this piss, he said. I want a Jack Daniels. Some instinct told me to stick with Lofty and his pals and see what they were worth, even though their rudeness about the drink would normally have made me avoid that sort of company.

I put the microphone to Lofty's mouth. He spat and snarled. I'm here fifty years now, and I don't like little fuckers from RTE here in Berlin. His cronies laughed. Lofty was a great laugh.

I asked a question that usually flatters people and makes them answer seriously. What advice would you give to anybody listening to this who is thinking of coming here to make their living? Lofty jumped in with a manic, snarling answer. Tell them bring a good cardboard box to sleep in. We all sleep in cardboard boxes. Lofty was hilarious.

What do you like about Berlin?

There's plenty whores here. You get a good woman for forty marks and you don't have to buy her drink or fuck all. Plenty of riding here in Berlin.

Where do you find the whores?

Oranienburgerstrasse. Just outside the door. Forty marks they do fucking anything for you.

I was getting out now. I had enough on tape from Lofty and his pals. Just before leaving I saw the Polizei coming in with a man. I asked Terry what was going on. Just a fellow caught travelling black on the U-Bahn, he said. It happens all the time. The man was in looking for his passport, which he needed to show to the police, and which was with his belongings behind the bar in the Oscar.

I had seen Irishmen travelling black, as they called it, on the public transport system as long as I had been coming to Germany, but it still amazed me the way Irishmen wouldn't pay the meagre train fare of three marks. If you can get away without paying, then you would be mad to pay. That seems to be their thinking. The German fare-paying system presumes honesty on the part of the traveller. There's nothing to stop you getting on the U-Bahn without buying and stamping your ticket. Chances are that you will not be challenged by the staff. Now one Irishman had been caught and was going to be fined. The fine isn't much, only forty marks, so men continue to risk the fine and the inconvenience and humiliation of being taken down to the police station for a few hours.

I left the Oscar and crossed the road and tramlines. I was staying in a place opposite the pub. It was a shabby building, like so many in former East Berlin. My room had only a bed and handbasin and I had to share the toilet and bathroom with the rest of the landing. At eighty-five marks per night, men told me, I was being robbed. The landlord – I think he was Turkish – was a rude bastard but I took the place because, when I arrived in Berlin earlier that day, I didn't have much time to look for anywhere else. Besides, the location suited me, straight across from the Oscar Wilde.

I opened the window of my room to get the last rays of the evening sun. Looking down Oranienburgerstrasse, I could see Lofty's whores. The nearest one, with her back to me, was wearing a short jacket and seemed to be wearing no knickers, only stockings and suspenders and, I would guess, a G-string. She was eye-catching. The whores of Berlin are glamorous and healthy-looking, not like the pathetic junkies you see on Benburb Street in Dublin. I can well imagine that a man coming out of the Oscar would spend forty marks on a woman to brighten up his weekend in Berlin and escape from the enforced male company of the rest of his week.

I put on my headphones and played back the tape. A good sound quality, I noted with satisfaction. In a noisy place like that pub you get good quality by keeping the record level low and holding the microphone close to the mouth of the interviewee. That makes the voice predominate over the background noise. I was listening for Lofty. There it was, all the rubbish he was talking about cardboard boxes and that. Then I got to the bit on whores. The rest of his ramblings I wouldn't broadcast but, on the whores, he knew what he was talking about. I would put his whore comments in my programme and to hell with him if that caused him embarrassment back in Ireland. Fuck you, Lofty. I'll make you sorry you crossed me.

Later on I took a walk and came across another Irish pub. It was called the Irish Times. The bar manager was a really nice Cork woman named Eileen whom I had met in Berlin a few years before, when she worked in the Oscar. Eileen made me welcome, then told me there had been a lot of trouble over my last programme. One of the women I interviewed had fallen out with her mum and dad when they heard their daughter's well-informed views on German men and their sexual appetites.

The Irish Times was a much quieter place than the Oscar Wilde. Mainly Germans here. The food was good and the live music was gentle. Then, after awhile, a group of young Irishmen got steadily noisier. They were shouting nonsense. One was imitating an upper-class English voice. Ready, aim, fire. Shoot the fuzzy-wuzzies. It was Skippy and his brothers, Eileen told me. They come to Berlin most weekends and go mad on drink. Eileen brought me over and introduced me.

Skippy was boastful and wanted to impress me, the man from RTE. He wore his mobile phone ostentatiously and went on about how many big contracts he had in Germany and how many men he had working for him. I suppose when he left Ireland he had nothing. Now he had money and importance here in Germany.

Skippy told me about Spremberg, the little town where he was working in recent months. It was about two hundred kilometers away, near the border with Poland. A new power station was being built. The Schwarze Pumpe. Thousands of immigrant workers were there, including a number of Irish. I took notes and said I would see him in a few days.

I sat back up at the bar. Awhile later, one of Skippy's brothers keeled over from his stool. There was a loud clunk as the man's head hit the tiled floor. There was blood. I got up to help. I crouched down by the injured man. Skippy turned to me and shouted into my face to get away. I saw, then, a flash of Skippy's violent temper, which I would learn a lot more about in the days to come. The injured man was helped out by his brothers and they left.

Awhile later Eileen, who knew I was a musician, asked me if I would play a few songs. The booked musician, an Aussie, cheerfully surrendered his guitar to me and took a rest. When the German audience learned I was from Ireland they were delighted. Can you, please, play Viskeys in ze Jar? I played the song for them and they sent me over drinks. It was like being back in Connemara.

Spremberg, a few days later

I took the train to Cottbus, a city about a hundred kilometers
south of Berlin, and then a train east to Spremberg, all the
way to the Polish border. It was like a journey back in time. A
lot of the railway engines and rolling stock in former East
Germany are old. Not like the modern transport system of the
West. As we got close to Poland, I noticed that the names of
the railway stations were in two languages. One was German
and the other I guessed, mistakenly, to be Polish. In fact, I
would learn, it was Sorabian, also called Wendish. It's a Slavic
language spoken in this part of Germany.

The sun was setting when the train got to the small, rural-
looking railway station in Spremberg. It was a town typical of
former East Germany. Lots of apartment blocks that many
Westerners would describe as "drab" but that would still put
the Dublin apartments of Ballymun or St Michael's, Inchicore,
or Mayfield in Cork to shame. Germans don't scrawl graffiti
on the walls or smash bottles on the footpaths or dump litter
or throw shitty nappies out the windows of their flats. As well
as that, East European working-class housing compares well
to what was western working-class housing during the first
century or more of western industrialisation. The
development of modern industry under working-class
dictatorship had its advantages for the workers.

I walked down a dark road through forest into the centre
of the town. It was a beautiful, picture-postcard place. There
were little old churches with bell-towers and houses with
fairy-tale roofs. I booked into a guesthouse, which was
comfortable and much better value than the hole I had left
behind in Berlin. Then I went looking for the pub Skippy had
told me about. It was called the Rats Kellar so I knew it
would be in the town square. I had learned in Germany and

159

in Denmark that rats means the rate house or town hall and I knew that kellar meant cellar. Sure enough, there was the Rats Kellar down the steps below some municipal buildings in the centre of town.

It was a small pub. Skippy wasn't there. I sat up at the horseshoe-shaped bar and ordered a Pils. A big, black-haired, bearded man in his late 30s was sitting opposite me, joking with the barmaid and breaking into what I took to be hearty German laughter. Two workmen who might have been Polish sat next to me. After awhile, I turned to these men and used a bit of German that I had found useful in the many previous times I had worked in this country. Sind Irisharbeiten hier? The two men were surprised by my question and shrugged.

No, they knew of no Irish workers in the town. The big man opposite me looked up and took notice. He winked a hello at me with a look that was a mixture of intrigue, puzzlement, suspicion and amusement. He continued to study me across his drink over the next few minutes. I got up, walked around the horseshoe bar and introduced myself. Guten tag. Ich com aus Irland.

The big man answered me in a strong, west of Ireland voice. C'mere boy, there's no way you're here looking for the shtart. Not with hands like yours you're not.

I told him who I was and what I was doing in Spremberg. He was pleased to meet me. He was a good radio listener back in Ireland and he knew my work well. His name was John. When I asked him about Skippy a look of pain crossed his face. If Skippy and his friends were allowed in the Rats Keller, he said, it was the last pub in town they weren't barred from. I'll give you a story, said Big John. Drink up and come with me.

We walked along the town to a pub called Der George. It was a young people's pub. Loud music and disco lights. Big

John spoke to the publican, a very attractive, well-dressed woman who knew John and was pleased to see him. My German was good enough to understand that John was explaining to her who I was and what I was doing. Then John introduced me to her. Tina spoke good, if strongly-accented, English.

"Vee haf no Irish here. Vee haf too much . . . kampf (fighting, John helped us) . . . with the Irish. And what I don't understand is that Irishmen fight with womans."

Tina's voice was raised in incredulity at the behaviour of the Irish. I asked her to explain what had happened so she called over two of her bar staff, a young black man from Greece and a local young woman. The woman had stitches over her eye. The Greek man spoke some English. No Irish here any more, he said. Then a long-haired youth joined us. He was the boyfriend of the injured bar-worker and he had been beaten up, too, in the incident some weeks before.

The long-haired man spoke German and John translated. It wasn't the first fight involving Skippy and his gang, but it had been the worst. It was after a lot of drink and the Irish went mad. Skippy hit the young woman with a bottle, splitting her open above the eye.

I asked Tina if the other immigrant workers in town, the Poles, the Turks, the English, ever caused trouble.

"Vee haf no problem with the English. Only with the Irish."

When John could see that I was suitably shaken by what I had heard, he asked me to come with him to another pub. Pugsley's was up a hill on the edge of town. It was a quiet place. One of the windows was boarded up. It had a bare light bulb and bare walls. Not a bit like Der George. Middle-aged men sat playing cards. Pugsley's reminded me of the sort of pub that was common in Ireland when I was a child.

Pugsley, the publican, was a young man with glasses and a fat face. He looked sombre as John spoke with him. Then he turned to me and, in good English, he asked me, curtly and without smiling, to wait a minute. Pugsley went to a room out the back where there was a television on. He spoke there with a young woman who got up and, with the help of a stick, limped into the pub. She had two black eyes which I guessed, correctly, were a side effect of the blow that had skinned the bridge of her nose. Pugsley introduced her to me. She was his wife.

Frau Pugsley sat down and spoke into my microphone. She spoke a German-Sorabian mixture (weeks later, back in Ireland, even good German-speakers in RTE could understand only small parts of the tape I made with Frau Pugsley). Pugsley translated for me but a lot of what his wife said needed no translation. She gestured with a head-butt to explain what had happened to her nose. Then she rolled up her sleeves to show bruising to her forearms, then she pointed to her injured leg. The stitches to the back of her head were explained by pointing to the wooden cues over at the pool table.

There were some words I did understand. She knew the names of the Irishmen who had attacked her. I was getting familiar with these names. Der Skippy und der Thomas und der Patrick. There was also a character, Der Cubischer. What had a Cuban got to do with it?

Pugsley explained. There was a big Cuban fellow living in town. He used to have a job here when the communists ran this place. Now he was doing very little except drink. The Cuban did arm-wrestling for bets. In Pugsley's, the night of the fight, he beat Skippy and company. When they wouldn't pay there was a row. Frau Pugsley intervened so Skippy attacked her. About eight Irishmen were involved in all.

Pugsley got his wife out into the back room and abandoned his pub to the Irish. They smashed the window and anything else they could find. Pugsley brought me out to the backyard and showed me broken chairs, tables and pool cues. Looking at the splintered wood, I could only try to imagine the level of mad anger that was unleashed that night.

I was stunned into silence by the time we went back into the bar. It suited me to let John and Pugsley keep the conversation in German. John said there were more places he could bring me to where the Irish were barred. I said no, thank you, I'd seen enough. Let's have a drink.

I bought a round of drinks for the whole pub, about twenty people in all, on RTE. Pugsley obliged me with a receipt. He told his customers who the drinks were from and who I was. I bought the drinks, I think, because of the sense of shame I was feeling. It was a gesture to say sorry for the behaviour of my fellow-countrymen and an attempt to mend relations between the Irish and these Sorabian-Germans, or whatever it is they like to be known as.

One of the card-players came and joined us. He was a lean, good-looking, balding man in his mid-40s. A sort of Sean Connery look-alike. He had a ready smile and a strong handshake. Thanks for the drink, he said. He spoke with a slow Derry accent. Big John introduced me to the man known as Derry Danny. Derry Danny said he would like to speak to me on the record so I took out my microphone. He said he was too ashamed to go into most pubs in Spremberg these days. It's a "keine Irish" policy in pubs here now, he said, and he didn't feel up to trying to explain to the locals that he was not one of the trouble-makers from the Skippy gang. Pugsley had stayed friends with him so he drank here.

Pugsley and his wife were good publicans, Danny said. When the Irish first came the Pugsleys made them welcome.

They got a map to see where Ireland was. Then they got in sports channels on the telly and learned what food the Irish would like. The problem was, said Derry Danny, that, like a lot of publicans who were new to the job, the Pugsleys were having to cope with all the trash of the town who were trying out their pub because they were barred from everywhere else.

Derry Danny was two years in Germany. He had seen his wife back in Derry only twice in those two years. And do you find that hard on your marriage, Danny? He pointed over to a woman about his own age who was sitting now at the card table. Derry Danny looked at me and spoke deliberately into the microphone. If you can't be with the one you love, love the one you're with.

The next day I dialed the mobile number that Skippy had given me a few days before when I met him in Berlin. When Skippy answered he didn't seem to remember who I was. Then he told me wasn't in Spremberg any more. I said I had met Pugsley. There was silence. Who? Pugsley, I said, the publican in Spremberg. I met his wife, too. Silence again. He said he didn't know them. Then he hung up.

That evening I met Big John with a couple of Irish friends who were renting a house with him. We went for something to eat. It was a place that the Skippy gang had trashed. I had gathered, at this stage, that John and anybody with him was welcome in all the bars. Big John spoke good German and seemed to be well-liked everywhere.

I told my friends that I had spoken on the phone to Skippy that morning and that he claimed he was out of town. They said that was possibly true as he had knocked a lot of men in Spremberg and they were after him for their money. Also, even though there were only two policemen in Spremberg, both middle-aged men who had been here for the years that this was just a quiet little town, it was possible that by now the Polizei had acted on the complaints they had got and that they were looking for Skippy.

Out of the restaurant, we queued up at a public phone to call our respective wives or partners in Ireland. There was an Englishman using the phone ahead of us. It was an open-air, side-of-the-road phone so we could hear what was being said. The Englishman didn't take any notice of us as we fell silent and listened. He probably didn't realise that we were English-speakers. Clearly, he was talking to the woman in his life. Heathrow, tomorrow, he said. Park the car in some quiet bit of the car park. No knickers. No, on second thoughts, no skirt or knickers. Just a coat. Then we'll have a quickie in the car park and a proper one when we get back home.

I think we were all feeling giddy but we managed not to break into loud laughter. Listening to the Englishman made me feel happy. The joy of sex. Clearly, he fancied this woman like crazy and he couldn't wait to be with her. I was glad for him. Glad he was getting away from this enforced, unnatural company of men. He hung up the phone and walked past us adjusting the front of his pants. When we got to the pub we laughed ourselves stupid.

Some days later, Dresden

I had the names of two Irish pubs in Dresden but I found the real Irish pub as soon as I got off the train. It was evening time when I arrived. A group of men sat around tables in the station foyer drinking bottles of beer from the cafe/bar. One of them called out to me in a Cork accent. Hey, giss a loan of your hat, will you?

It wasn't the first time that my eccentric-looking, broad-rimmed hat had got me an introduction to people I wanted to meet. The young Corkman couldn't have known that I was an English-speaker. It was just that, in his drunkenness, he was entertaining himself by shouting at passers-by. The Corkman had tightly cropped, bleached blonde hair. He was bruised and grazed about his eyes and head. I leaned over the other men and put my hat on the Corkman's head. I need the hat more than you do, I said, making a joke as I revealed my baldness. The men laughed.

There were about a dozen Irish there in all and two or three English. The Corkman told me exactly where he was from in east Cork. I told him I was from Cobh and he shook my hand with the exaggerated friendliness of a drunk. Just down the road from you, boy. The Corkman was beyond interviewing. That would have to wait at least until the next day when he might have sobered up, but I introduced myself to the other men and took out my tape-recorder. I left it on the table in front of me as I knew it would be a while before I would be able to use it. The men exchanged suspicious glances. I could see this was going to be difficult.

The men were working in a city-centre site just across from the station. This was their local after work. As we chatted, I dropped as many names as I could of men I had interviewed in Berlin and in Spremberg. Some of the men knew Big John and thought highly of him. Then I mentioned Skippy and the men sat up and took notice.

Where is the bastard? Is he still in Spremberg? A number of the men had been knocked by Skippy. I turned on my tape-recorder and they started talking with a passion. One Galwayman with an effeminate voice had lost almost three weeks' pay a few months before when he worked for Skippy in Berlin. There was hurt in this man's voice. I felt sorry for him. It must be awful to work hard for weeks, as these men do, and then not be paid.

The Galwayman said why he had come to Germany. His Irish wife in London left him for a big black man. There were no black men in Germany and that's why he liked it here. The other men joined in, warming to the subject. England was ruined by blacks. The Germans hadn't made the same mistake of letting blacks in. The blacks in London are terrible. They walk down the street and expect you to get out of the way.

You probably think we're all terrible racists, said one of the men. (He pronounced it like "rayshists".) I said that nobody could tell them who they should like or not like. Then I got up to buy a round of drinks. We drank like Germans. Bottled beer by the neck.

One of the men was very drunk and I had barely a clue what he was saying to me. He kept shaking my hand and wouldn't let go. He was aged somewhere between forty and fifty, with a face like Miley out of the television programme *Glenroe*. His features were sagging with the effect of alcohol. He was dribbling through his rotten teeth. He spoke with a West Cork accent. He was saying something about the wet canteen being great.

The other men explained. On a German construction site you have a wet canteen and a dry canteen. The dry canteen is where you get a mid-morning cup of tea, which would be in keeping with the tradition of Irish building workers. The wet canteen is a German tradition. It's where you get a bottle of beer. Great for getting the dust out of your mouth. The Irish were taking quite well to this German custom of the wet canteen.

I asked the men if they thought it was dangerous to go up

scaffolding or to use machinery after drinking. They said there was no danger. It wasn't the beer that was to blame for all the accidents, they said. It was that the East German workers and the Poles didn't have the building experience of the Irish or English. A Polish man died on their site just a few days before. What happened was that lengths of steel for concrete reinforcement were being delivered by lorry. There wasn't a proper sling for lifting the load off the back of the truck so the Poles hooked up the hoist to the wires that were holding the lengths of steel together during transport. When the steel was lifted from the lorry the wires broke and the man was crushed.

Men who worked on the Schwarze Pumpe in Spremberg told me about horrific accidents. One man described seeing blood hosed off from an area where a man had just fallen to his death. Then the concrete was poured in with the dead man's blood still spattered on the steel re-enforcing frame.

I said to the men that there must be accidents involving Irishmen, too. They couldn't think of any fatalities but, after a while, every man seemed to recall an Irishman who was either home in England or Ireland, having suffered a broken back or some other injury that would mean he could never work again.

The effeminate Galwayman spoke some more. He had a glum voice. Back to the tin can tonight. Living like a dog. Up again for six. A bowl of water for your face. Then back working again.

The tin can meant a container, as in container traffic. These are converted with doors and windows cut out and bunks installed. Up to six men might live in one of these tin cans. You see them stacked around the big building sites. There are ladders up to the upper stories.

One of the men asked me if I would like to see inside a
tin can. I said I would, but then the other men argued about
it, saying they might have a difficulty getting me past site
security. I said I would leave it for another time. I had done
enough work for one evening.

I stayed that night in a place the men directed me to, the
Red Cross hostel across the road from the railway station.
Apparently, if there have been no major accidents, the Red
Cross rooms are available for paying customers such as
myself. I set my watch alarm for 5.30 a.m. The men told me
they were going to work at six and that they would have
breakfast in the railway station.

If the men can do it, I can do it too, I thought. It wasn't
easy, though, getting up at that time when you'd had a few
beers the night before. I crossed the road in the early
morning darkness. Dresden was already coming awake. Miley
and a Connemara man whom they called "the Connie" were
at a kiosk just inside the doorway of the station, drinking
beers before going to work. I took out my tape-recorder. I
noted with satisfaction that there were loud station
announcements being made as we spoke. This would sound
good when I broadcast this stuff on the radio in a few weeks
time. It would give a strong sense of place to the listeners.

Miley was marginally more coherent after his few hours'
sleep but he still wasn't sober. He was a shuttering carpenter,
he told me. (He pronounced his trade as I have heard Irish
builders in London pronounce it before. "Carpenter" is said
like "car*pen*ter".) He went to Scotland when he was fourteen
and worked in London after that. He was single and went
home to West Cork every two years or so, to his brother who
had a farm. He would be going there at Christmas and he
would see his nieces and nephews.

Miley shrugged when I asked him if he would ever go back to Ireland and perhaps buy a place with his savings. He didn't seem to want to think about the future. I wondered, but didn't ask, if Miley had any savings left from all his years of earning big money in London and now in Germany. It would be hard to spend all your money on drink while working in Germany. The men were earning more than there was time to spend. But a determined drinker could take weeks off at a time or blow all his money back in England. Miley was a determined drinker. Before too many more years go by, I can see Miley ending up in a London doss house like so many Irishmen before him.

The Connie, a middle-aged man with a cloth cap and red nose, had said nothing to me the evening before. He just smiled shyly whenever I went near him with the microphone and, this morning, he was no different. Are you married?, I asked the Connie. He smiled, shook his head and spoke a nearly breathless "no". Are you living long in Germany? A flicker of the eyes, a slight click of the tongue. No answer. The Connie barely ever made eye-contact.

I asked Miley about living in the tin can. Tin city, they call it. There's Irish, English, Portuguese, Poles, Yugoslavs. There are showers on site but, Miley told me, he doesn't use them. He has a basin of cold water next to his bed and first thing in the morning, he puts his feet in the basin to wake up. (I didn't understand that either. I'm only telling you what he said.)

The rest of the men came out of the cafeteria and collected Miley and the Connie on their way to work. All the men were in good form as they greeted me. Will you be around later? they asked me. It's the weekend. We'll have a good night tonight. Then they went off towards the site, their cigarettes glowing as they crossed the road in the pre-dawn darkness.

I walked into the city. I aimed for the palaces and cathedrals of the city centre. I knew that most of this city had been rebuilt since it was flattened during the war years. There were east European-style apartments everywhere that were built, I am sure, during the years of communism. The old, historic centre of the city has been re-built as it once was. That rebuilding is still going on today. I crossed the Elbe. I have never seen such a broad, mighty river. That was some bridge to cross.

I got breakfast at a cafe on the river bank. Brot mit kasse und cafe. I got bread with cheese and a cup of coffee largely because I knew how to ask for it. In this part of Germany, you need to speak German, unlike in the West, where it's almost impossible to try to speak it because the Germans will answer you in English. Here in the East, for decades, the language learned by everybody in school was Russian. English was a third language learned by only a few.

A few hours later I wandered into the railway station again. The young Corkman with the bleached hair and scratched face was there again, along with a few more. The Corkman told me he had taken the last few days off work because he was depressed after being knocked. He was in the railway station because the Irish pub didn't open early enough. He introduced me to his friends. A young Kilkenny man and two Londoners. One Londoner was aged about twenty and the other was about forty. The older man was rough-looking, with a shaven head. This is Skinhead Stan, the Corkman said. Stan, meet Paddy. He's a journalist from Ireland.

Stan looked up from the his English tabloid newspaper. Stan's face hardened. So you're a journalist are you? Well why don't you write something on the farking child support farking agency? That's why I'm here working for farking Fritz, innit? My wife wants my money even though she's living wiv annuvah geezer. She can fark orf. He can farking pay for 'er and the kids. And the farking journalists always stand up for the women, don'ey?

I said nothing. I just nodded along. Skinhead Stan was working himself into fury. It was like watching a furnace with an open door with the flames being fanned into a blaze. After a while I thought I had better say something in case he thought I was being smart by not answering.

Well, Stan, I'm sorry that you've had that experience from the Child Support Agency. There's a lot of people who would question the way the agency works . . .

You're farking sorry, are you mate? It's all right for farking you, innit? I've met Irish blokes here who pay fark all for their kids. It's only farking England . . .

It went on and on. The Corkman was laughing and began talking gently and nudging the much larger Englishman who was ranting on regardless. Stan, shut up. You fucking Brit, shut fucking up, you're doing my head in. Hey, you Brit. You're talking to an Irishman there, show a bit of respect.

Stan finally noticed the Corkman insulting him. He stopped his ranting and turned to the smaller man. I held my breath. Stan exhaled in embarrassed laughter. Fark orf, mate. 'Ere, it's my round. What are you 'aving, mate?

Stan went to get us all beers and the other men told me not to worry about him. He was a good boss to have, they said. Stan looked a bit chastened when he joined us again. He seemed to realise that he had been out of order. We chatted now in a more relaxed way. It turned out that he and the younger Londoner were from Eastcote. That was where I lived as a child. We talked a bit about shops and street names and swimming at the Ruislip Lido as kids. My other memories were of the local Catholic church and Catholic school, neither of which meant anything to Stan.

Stan apologised for his earlier bad temper. I asked Stan if he had ever been knocked. They all warmed to this one. They got their revenge the last time they were knocked. When the sickening truth sank in that they had been done out of money, they got their own back by filling the U-bends of all the wash-hand-basins with cement. Then they punctured all the water pipes. This destruction wouldn't be noticed until the mains were switched on after which all the floors would have to come up again. You have to teach Fritz, said Stan, that you don't fuck with the Paddies.

I asked the Corkman what happened to his face. He told me that a few days before, he fell getting out of a tram. He was drunk. His German girlfriend of eighteen months left him after that accident. He had gone on the beer since. She was a hairdresser and had a nice flat in which he had been living. She told him that she couldn't stand his drinking any more. That's the trouble with the German women. They want to boss you around.

The explanation for the Corkman's bleached hair was clear to me now. It was a fashion that wasn't common among Irish builders. I also understood now why the Corkman was so much more drunk than the other men the evening before. Men like Miley and the Connie are an exception in that they can drink continuously and still work. Most men are more like the Corkman. To get that drunk by tea-time you need to have taken the day off work.

Your girlfriend did your hair?

He nodded and began to get maudlin. He missed her very much and wanted to be back with her. And now he had nowhere to live so Stan was putting him up.

Are you in a tin can, Stan?

No, said Stan, I don't live like that, in with a load of blokes farting. I rent a house.

The Corkman said he would never live in a tin can again after what happened last year. He got drunk at a disco and was taken outside by the bouncers and beaten up. Some hours later he was discharged from hospital and, with a bandaged head, he went back to his tin can to lie down. Later, the other lads, who hadn't missed him, came home steaming drunk. They climbed into their bunks. A few minutes later, the Corkman felt warm liquid trickling down on him through the mattress of the bunk above. The fellow up top had pissed the bed. The Corkman dived up out of his sick bed in anger and, with an almighty shove from below, he threw the top bunk, man, mattress, sheets, wanking books and all, out onto the floor. Never again would he live in a tin can.

I asked the men how to get to the Slyne Head, an Irish pub I had heard of. The Corkman laughed. I wouldn't see him there, he said. He was barred. He was in a row with a fellow so he bought a gun. This was a gun of the sort that fired gas canisters. It would have been used by the old East German police for riot control. (It was easy to buy guns in this part of Germany. The disintegration of the Warsaw Pact armies had left all sorts of weaponry on the market as soldiers sold off the only commodities they had.) The Corkman went into the Slyne Head with his gun and his girlfriend. He had meant only to use the gun to frighten a fellow with but,

174

downstairs in the toilets, the gun went off, causing the whole pub to fill with riot-control gas. After this incident, the German boss at the Slyne Head was angry. He barred the Corkman for two weeks. Through pride, the Corkman never went back.

I got a taxi to the Slyne Head. That's where I caught my first sight of Tonto. He was outside the pub, surrounded by a group of teenage German girls. Tonto was aged about thirty. He was small with long hair, a beard and big bulging eyes. He was doing something like a Maori dance on the pavement, contorting his ugly face to make it even more hideous than it naturally was. He was thrusting a long pole sort of thing in front of him that I learned later was something he used in his work for sticking tiles on ceilings. Tonto spoke to the German girls in an uncompromising Dublin accent and used what must have been, to the Germans, impenetrable Dublin expressions. Get up the yard. That kind of thing. The women loved it. Tonto irritated me from the start.

I told Tonto what I was doing in Dresden. Oh brother, I could tell you a few things, brother, he said. I could make you one of the top journalists in Europe. I done time in the 'Joy.

Tonto looked at me to make sure that I was suitably awed by his prison record. He seemed to think that I had never before come face-to-face with an ex-prisoner.

But, Tonto went on, you'd need to have your price right before I spoke to you about that.

I told Tonto that I wouldn't want him to say anything to me that he might regret and that might lead to his extradition back to Ireland. A man like him needed to be cautious.

Tonto seemed flattered by that but it wasn't enough for him. Did I want to know what he was in prison for?

No Tonto, best not to tell me.

Ah, I know you journalists, always looking for information. You're trying to trick me now into saying something. Looking for an exclusive.

No, Tonto. I wouldn't play a trick on you. Tell you what, some information I would like, might you know where I can get a room for the night?

Tonto said he'd organise something for me. He left me for a minute with the German girls then he came back with a key and told me I could have his room above the pub cos tonight he wasn't going to be using it, you know yourself brother, he said, winking and making eyes towards one of the girls. He charged me twenty marks and told me not to say anything to the boss. There's clean sheets in the cupboard. Just one rule. No wanking in his bed.

One of the Germans gasped and giggled, then her friends asked Tonto vot vas vanking? I left Tonto to explain.

Later that evening the Slyne Head was busy. It was full of Germans. I spoke with some of them, two women and a man, all well-dressed. They come to the Irish pub to speak English. They were professional people of some sort. Next year they would go to Ireland on holidays. It would be their first visit. They were very interested in Irish culture. The Irish and the Germans have a lot in common, they felt. I smiled and nodded along. They meant no harm.

Then in came Miley, the Connie and a whole lot more of the railway station gang. It was nice to see them all. Miley came over to shake my hand. The Connie did the same, barely looking at me, as usual. Miley shook hands with my German friends, too. Miley looked washed and ironed. I'm sure he was glad to get out of his working clothes from this, Saturday evening, until Monday morning. Miley and the

Connie squashed in next to me. Then Miley shook hands again with the Germans who looked puzzled by this Irish behaviour of serial handshakes. Oh, no. Miley's pissed again.

I told Miley that my German friends were going to Ireland next year but there was no point talking to him. Miley was in his own world, that nirvana that alcoholics strive for. The Germans got back to asking me things about Ireland then Miley emerged from nirvana once again and was sticking his hand out for more handshakes. He was nudging them, his face drooping with drink, spit flecking his lips. The Germans got up to leave. Miley didn't even notice that he had driven my friends away. The other Irishmen took the free seats. Miley's drunken carry-on was something they were used to and could cope with. Irishmen are at ease with Irish culture.

I walked across the pub and Tonto saw me. He shouted to me from among his women friends. No wanking in my bed. I'll be checking the sheets.

I bought Tonto and his friends a drink and sat down to relax but Tonto wouldn't give me a break. Don't you be pumping me for information now, brother. See, I can't go back to Dublin. I'd be extradited if they knew I was here. I'm a wanted man. I have a wife and child in Dublin but I'm not allowed to see them because of what the police in Ireland did to me.

Really, Tonto, what did the police do?

I'm up for GBH. There was a fellah interfering with children so I gave him my own justice. There now, you're after me for information again.

I tried to look as if I believed Tonto but I doubted his story. Very likely he had done time in prison but his story of

177

bashing a molester was just too convenient for his present needs in Germany. He was the only Dublin man I had met all week. He was living now among rural Irishmen. Culchies don't regard a spell in prison with the same indifference as working-class Dubliners do. So Tonto needed to explain the prison sentence by finding a crime that would have widespread male approval. Bashing a molester was a story that suited this purpose exactly.

Tonto was hard to take for too long. I was feeling drunk anyhow and it was time to go to bed. Don't worry, Tonto. I won't wank in your sheets. I'm too drunk now even for that.

Sunday morning was sad. A thirty-nine-year-old Scot, John Gallacher from Glasgow, was knocked. I found him in his room upstairs above the Slyne Head, sitting with his head in his hands. Not only had the subbies gone without paying him. They had taken his tools. The subbies who knocked him were two brothers from Ireland. John showed me the "Dear John" letter that they left him. Sorry to do this to you, John, but your work was really not up to standard. We have taken your tools to cover the investment we made in you. If you contact Horst, you will find that he owes us money and you can have that.

John Gallacher contacted Horst but, of course, the German had already paid the Irishmen for the work he contracted. This is not my problem, said Horst.

John traveled with me on the tram into the city. I let him talk. It was all for his wife and the two wee lassies at home, he kept saying. He came here just four weeks ago to make money. He persuaded his wife that it was for the best. Now weeks of work had been wasted. How could he tell his wife how he had been made such a fool of? He trusted the

Irishmen. I cannay think how two fellow-Breet-ish workers could do that to you. He was ready to get the next flight home to Glasgow.

We reached the station and the usual gang were there plus a lot more English and Irish whom I didn't know. The men were good to John when they heard what happened. They poured lots of drink into him and told him other stories about being knocked. Then along came the man known as Armagh Mick, the man I had heard of back in Berlin. He was middle-aged, small and tough-looking. He told John that the two brothers who knocked him were based in San Francisco until recently. They can go back there, said Mick, cos let me tell you, them two boys won't get a living in this town again, or anywhere else in this country if I have anything to do with it. I think Armagh Mick's northern accent made his solemn declaration against the San Francisco brothers sound all the more ominous. You know what I mean. Northerners have that aura about them.

Big John was there, down from Spremberg for the weekend. It was good to see him again. We greeted each other like long-lost pals, even though it was just a few days since we'd met. Being in a foreign country does that to people.

The beers were coming down in crates. I was chatting with a few Londoners, standing around a table. One man was aged about fifty, an aged hippy with long hair and a beard. He was in the building industry all his life, he told me, and he loved it. He met characters all over the world. Now, here in Dresden, he was on his fourth wife, a Czech woman half his age.

There was a disturbance from the Irish area. I couldn't

believe it. It was the Connie. Over the last few days he had said nothing. Now he was on his feet shouting and waving his arms at his crotch. If she has a fanny she should keep her fucking fanny. I've a mickey and I don't want a fucking fanny. That's sick.

The other men were shushing him and telling him to sit down but he wouldn't shut up. What had happened was that he had come across something in one of the English tabloids about somebody wanting a sex-change operation.

At last this silent, middle-aged Irishman had found something he had a strong opinion on. One of the German bar staff came over to him. Britisher, Britisher, he snapped, waving his hand at the Connie to make him sit down. The other men finally got the Connie to order. They were laughing. Miley was the only one not noticing. He was on the seat next to the Connie and was asleep, his beer bottle held limply in his hand.

I went over to the phone booth to make a call to Dublin. It was Sunday morning and Deirdre was still in bed when she answered. Very quickly she had me wishing I was there with her. As I spoke with Deirdre, I was looking out of the phone booth at Miley, still asleep and now with a long dribble coming from his mouth. I had enough of the company of men. I told Deirdre I would see her very soon.

After my phone call, I stood apart from the men for awhile. All these drinkers. So many broken marriages. I remembered the men in the Oscar saying to me that it was working in the building industry, always away from home, that led to their drinking and marriage break-ups. Now I believed the opposite to be as much the case. Many of them were here because they didn't want a home life with a woman. They were prepared to live in tin cans so long as they could earn big money and spend it all in the pub. Just as paedophiles are attracted to the priesthood, so too, alcoholics are attracted to the building industry.

My thoughts were interrupted by a friendly London voice. All right, mate. It was Skinhead Stan. He was in chirpy form, different to the black humour I had found him in the day before. Stan said he wouldn't join me for a drink because he was about to get the train to Prague. A contract he was hoping for had fallen through but he wasn't going to worry. He was going to take a few days off work and forget about his troubles. Prague was his favourite place. He loved it for its cheap drink and cheap whores. Stan asked me to turn on my tape recorder. He gave me a little bit of poetry.

My name is Stan

And I don't give a fuck

Cos I'm off to Prague to get me cock sucked.

The last line was spoken in a cheerful, upbeat way. I rate Stan's poetry along with that of Myles na gCopaleen. Just as in Myles, when all has gone wrong all around you, salvation can be reached for in the form of a pint of plain being your only man, so too, Stan had his salvation in Prague. I'm off to Prague to get me cock sucked. I often say Stan's lines to myself these days if I'm feeling down. I find it has an uplifting effect on my spirits. You should try it.

The next morning Big John gave me a lift as far north as Cottbus. We had a drink in the station bar in Cottbus then John headed east for Spremberg and I took the train to Berlin. I enjoyed the journey. I was happy with my week's work and I was looking forward to being in Dublin that night. I was finished with the company of men.

Chapter Eight

ASHLEY

District Court, The Bridewell, Dublin;
July 1996

I'm after being up in court for a load of things. This morning I'm up for a one-ninety-nine hair clip I robbed out of Penny's. The last time was for soliciting. Prostitution.

Ashley was aged twenty-four. Her hair was tied back, showing off her pock-marked cheeks. Her face was thin. Her body was slight, wasted-looking. Her Dublin accent wasn't as strong as is usual with junkies. It turned out she was from Rathfarnham, a Dublin suburb with a gentler accent than that of the inner city.

My cameraman, Gerard Cannon, was standing on my right, filming over my shoulder. We were in the first thirty minutes of working together. We had just a few hours to make a television programme before getting back to our usual day jobs. I had scrounged the camera from RTE for a few days. With Ashley, I knew I'd made a good start. She was an exceptional interviewee. The sort that you never forget.

Is there a strong reason why you work as a prostitute?

I do it for money for drugs. Heroin.

When did you start work as a prostitute?

It was before last Christmas I started working at Benburb

Street. I wanted to get the money for the kids. They're in care and I wanted them to have nice things for Christmas. I'm homeless now and I want to have enough money to get out of the B&B and get my own place.

Ashley answered every question clearly and carefully. She wanted to do a good job for television.

I know I'll probably end up back in Mountjoy. I tried to hang myself there. I tore up the sheets and twisted them round the bars of the window but I couldn't do it.

A group of travellers came out of the court. The oldest man was drunk and started acting the fool behind Ashley, waving at the camera and shouting something incoherent. I said to Ger to keep filming. I wasn't making a fly-on-the-wall documentary. I was making a programme about what happens when you go to the Bridewell to interview people for television.

Ashley took her cue from me and ignored the drunk. She continued to answer my questions. But she found the next interruption much more interesting. A rough-looking young man barged his way into camera shot. He was waving a small brown-paper bag in his hand. Do you want to smoke some heroin? Ashley answered immediately. I do.

The young man wore a rucksack on his back. For some reason I still don't understand, he spoke with a stage-French accent. I am leaving Ireland today, he said. I am wanted for murder. I cut a man's throat in Limerick. But look, he cut me first. (He pulled down his shirt collar, showing the camera a frightful, fairly recent wound.) I have to finish all this heroin before I go to England. You come with me.

The fellow was mad. I didn't care about that, but I did care that he was taking Ashley away from me. She said she'd be back but I knew I was probably losing her because I had to leave very soon. I was producing RTE's *Today at Five* radio programme that afternoon and I needed to get to a meeting with colleagues by midday. Ger, too, had to get to Dublin Cable Television where he was working. We arranged to meet Ashley again at eight that evening. She went off around the corner to smoke her heroin. I didn't hold out much hope of seeing Ashley again. I felt I had lost her and that it could take months to find her again.

I got into RTE. It's a different world to that of the Bridewell. You get so used to looking at junkies in the Bridewell that you nearly forget that they don't look normal. It's a relief to be away from the courts and to see healthy-looking people again. My colleagues were relaxed and good-humoured. Not for them the endless stress of a life of drug addiction and crime.

Later, I met Ger Cannon outside the Bridewell as arranged. We waited an hour in the evening sunshine but there was no show from Ashley. Maybe she changed her mind, said Ger. No, I said. It was nothing as definite as that. It was like I have always found with underclass people in general and junkies in particular. They don't stick to arrangements. Their world goes from one crisis to another. They get arrested, they need drugs, they need money. They don't organise their day the way that you and I organise ours. Appointments mean very little in their lives. Ashley will talk to us again if we can only find her. I'll see you back here in the morning, Ger.

Deirdre was free from work the next day and she joined Ger and me outside the Bridewell. We got the familiar stories of the courts. Joyriders, shop-lifters and lots of junkies. One joyrider spoke to camera about getting bailed. To be released from prison this time he had to come up with £1000 cash bail. And where did you get that from?

Me ma.

So your mother has to come up with money to keep you

184

out of prison. Do you ever think about the upset you cause to her by getting into all this trouble?

Ah, yeah. Me ma and da would both be crying, coming up to see me in prison and all. But that won't stop me stealing cars.

A woman of about thirty-five with bobbed blonde hair spoke to us. She had been in the court to hand over tobacco to her husband who had been brought down from Mountjoy to the Bridewell to face more charges. The prison warden accepted the tobacco to give to him. And was she ever up in court herself?

My husband's a drug addict, she said, but I was only ever up for receiving stolen goods. If I would've haven to pay for them in the shops it would've costen me twice as much. (Her words "haven" and "costen" are a past tense, subjunctive construction in Dublin working-class speech.)

I went inside Court Four to try to spot any likely-looking candidates for interview. There was a young woman with long hair standing at the front. She stood silently as the judge, the prosecuting garda and her brief discussed her fate. She had a plastic Coke bottle sticking out of her jacket pocket. An obvious junkie. The screw-up bottle was, no doubt, full of methadone that she had bought on the street. This methadone (usually called "phye", short for Physeptone, the brand name) was needed to help her through the pains and sickness of being without heroin. I couldn't hear what was being said. As usual, it was very hard to hear what was going on in the court. But it didn't matter. The woman was taken down, her face impassive as she was escorted down the steps to the cells below. So much for my hopes of getting an interview.

Back outside the Bridewell I saw a man and a woman approaching. I recognised the man, a tall, scrawny, sick-looking fellow with rotten teeth. Colin, aged about thirty, was a junkie we had interviewed the day before. I noticed again how carefully Colin kept himself, despite his sick appearance. His denim jeans and jacket were washed. His hair was combed. His hands and nails were scrubbed clean. Then I realised I knew the woman, too. Her hair was down now, not tied back like the day before. It was Ashley.

Colin and Ashley were pleased to see us again. I hadn't realised the day before that there was a romance between these two people whom we had met and interviewed separately. Ashley said nothing about missing our arrangement the evening before. I doubt she even thought about it.

It was Colin who was up in court today. He would get a remand, he said. It was all for stupid things. Robbing out of houses and shops. Nothing serious, thank God.

After Colin came out of court, he and Ashley sat together on the Bridewell steps and I joined them, microphone in hand. I'll get a three-shot, said Ger.

Ashley was in her working clothes. When her jacket fell open, her belly was exposed. She wore a kind of bra-like top and long pants cut low on her hips. Just below the clasp to the front of her pants there was a circular opening about two inches in diameter, exposing even more of her lower belly. I noticed that she put her handbag on her lap to keep her belly hidden from the camera. She wore make-up that covered her pock-marked cheeks. She looked very different to the way she did the day before. Some people who got to see the final version of the video didn't realise that the prostitute we interviewed with her hair tied back and the one we interviewed the next day with her hair down were the same person.

I hate being a prostitute. I hope this goes on television

because I want my sisters to know that I'm sorry I robbed them and robbed their houses but that I needed money cos I have a habit. Now I don't have to go robbing any more. I can make me own money. I have six sisters and one brother and I'm the youngest and I'm the only black sheep and I'm sorry I don't talk to me family any more.

Ashley was crying. Colin had his arm over her as he lit her cigarette. I suggested that we all go for coffee. We picked Hughes's Pub, which is near the Bridewell. The five of us – Ashley, Colin, Ger, Deirdre and I – went in. I wondered whether or not we would be served. One look at Colin and you would check your belongings. But Frank, the barman in Hughes's, is a man I have been friends with for twenty years, from when I first lived in Dublin and he used to run a pub in Parliament Street. Frank made us welcome. When I explained what we were doing with the camera he found us a quiet area with good lighting. Frank does a bit of broadcasting himself on Anna Livia radio.

We got soup and sandwiches. Colin and Ashley barely touched the food. Junkies never seem to have much of an appetite. It was lunchtime and the pub was filling up with its usual mixture of customers from the courts. There were police, both uniform and plainclothes. There were prison officers. There were legal types and their criminal clients. A group of prison officers sat at the next table. Colin recognized one of them and began to call out to him. Mr. Murphy, sir, how are you?

Murphy barely responded but Colin persisted until he got a hello back for his troubles. Colin didn't seem to realise that Murphy wasn't interested in exchanging small talk with him. Mr Murphy was on my landing in the Joy, Colin told us.

For the camera, Colin and Ashley talked about their sets of children. Ashley hoped to get hers out of care soon. Colin was upset because he had to take an Aids test to help persuade a judge that he was fit to see his children. And do you have Aids, Colin?

Colin and Ashley had both taken tests and were both negative. We have Hepatitis, said Ashley, but that's just your liver. We'd love to get off drugs but the Corporation won't give us a place to live.

They explained that, at the moment, Ashley was in a B&B and Colin was sleeping rough in the Gorman. (The Gorman is the derelict building that was once the psychiatric hospital known as Grangegorman. A lot of homeless people sleep there.) Colin unzipped a small bag that he wore at his hip. It was full of toiletries. I have to use the toilets of pubs to wash in, said Colin. I can't live like this. Until we get a place to live, we can't get off drugs.

Typical junkies. They're always going to give up drugs but, in the meantime, somebody else is to blame for their ongoing drug habit. I felt sorry for them but I felt the anger that I have felt so often before in dealing with addicts.

Ashley said she had to go to work. She needed to raise another £80 that day for herself and Colin. I asked if we could come with her and she said yes, of course. As we got up to leave a policeman noticed Colin. The garda was a big, ruddy-faced man in his late forties. His face showed surprise at seeing the like of Colin in the pub. I'm not sure if he knew Colin, but he knew a junkie when he saw one. His eyes scanned Colin and the rest of us to see what we might have robbed. Then his gaze fell on Ashley and her bare lower belly. The policeman knew a whore when he saw one, too. His red face twisted into a sneer that was a mixture of lust and contempt.

Outside we got into Deirdre's car and made for Benburb Street. It was about five years since I last worked that street. I wondered if anything much had changed. I came here several times over the years with Frances Flynn, a junkie prostitute with Aids whom I was friends with from the time I first met her in July of 1990 until her death in January of 1993. Benburb Street is the rough end of the Dublin prostitution market. Most of the women here are junkies or alcoholics. They are often beer-bellied with tough, weathered faces. They make the Fitzwilliam prostitutes look glamorous.

Benburb Street women are cheap. I remember one of them, a middle-aged, sour-faced woman that Frances introduced me to, telling me her price. She said it like it was a street-seller's jingle. Fifteen for a ride with rubber, a tenner for a toss.

That particular woman wouldn't talk to me on tape but, she said, Margaret might. Here comes Margaret now. I saw Margaret coming towards us. They couldn't be serious that this woman was earning money here as a prostitute. She was heavy, middle-aged and dirty-looking with greasy hair. Her legs were swollen and lumpy at the lower calves. Her dirty toes stuck out through the slippers which she wore out here on the street. Most of all, I remember her walk. She had the heavy, swaying gait of a person in later middle-age. You would want to offer Margaret a seat if you saw her coming, not open your fly to her.

Margaret, I remember, wouldn't talk to me either. I didn't have much luck that day. Frances Flynn and her life-long friend Rose Waldron, now also dead, were my two great interviewees of Benburb Street who were always willing to talk to me.

I asked Ashley if she knew Frances or Rose. She didn't. They were already dead before Ashley started working here. They were probably already dead before Ashley became a drug addict. Ashley was one of the new generation of junkie-prostitutes, following in the footsteps of the like of Frances and Rose.

We reached Benburb Street. Deirdre pulled in the car across from Collins's Barracks. Ashley was in the front passenger seat. I sat behind Ashley, microphone in hand. Colin was next to me and Ger next to him. Ger focused on Ashley. Camera rolling, he said.

I charge twenty pounds for sex. That's for pene– how do you say it? Penetration. That's what all the women charge here. Usually we go to the Phoenix Park, or sometimes in the car. There's a deaf-and-dumb fellow is one of my regulars and we do it in the back of his van.

Have you ever been attacked while working here, Ashley?

Once with a knife and once with fists. The time with the fists, I was robbed. The time with the knife I was in the Phoenix Park and we got out and he told me to undress and kneel down in the grass. Then he came behind me and tried to put it in but he couldn't get it in. Then he started getting real angry.

Ashley was beginning to cry. I was getting a lot more detail than I had looked for when I asked the question. She had a faraway look in her face. In her mind she was back at that night in the Phoenix Park and she was going to tell it like it happened.

Next he had a knife and he put it in me . . . there . . . and he told me it was a knife and I grabbed me trousers and ran and kept running. It was only later that I knew he'd cut me when I saw me trousers was all blood.

(I'm looking back at the video as I write this now. Perhaps it was too explicit for broadcast, but I will never forget the effect of hearing this plain-spoken young woman telling it like it is for a prostitute on the streets when she was about to get out and face all this danger again. When I edited the video-tapes in RTE the technician with me left me in no doubt about her view. You have to leave that in, Paddy, she said. That's telling it like it is.)

Are you friends, Ashley, with any of the other women here?

That's Tina over there. She's been here longer than I have. She's nice but I never talk much when I'm here. The way I see it, time spent here is for working, not for talking.

Ger zoomed the camera in on Tina. When I looked at the close-up pictures afterwards I saw that Tina was tough-looking to the point of ugliness. She might have been as young as thirty but she was getting the leather-faced look of a Benburb Street woman. (In the final video package, I cut out the parts where Tina's face was visible, for obvious reasons.) Tina wore a ludicrously short skirt and boots. The overall effect at a distance was at least eye-catching. Up close, the whole effect was hideous. Poor Tina.

Ashley had to go to work and so did Ger and I. She got out of the car and we filmed her and Colin as they crossed the road and walked down the pavement next to the high wall of Collins's Barracks. Then they parted and Ashley kept walking. A car stopped almost immediately. The driver had passed Tina and picked up the much better-looking Ashley.

The driver and Ashley spoke for a few moments, then Ashley climbed in. The driver was a prosperous-looking man in his late forties. As he drove past, Colin noted the registration number on the back of a cigarette-packet and read it out to the camera. That's my job now, Paddy, said Colin. If Ashley gets attacked again, I'll have the number of the car and we'll be able to tell the police. It's not nice being known as a pimp, Paddy, but I do it to look after her.

Colin left us to wait up at Arbour Hill where Ashley always gets dropped back. He sat there on a step. I would like to have stayed there, too, so as to get Ashley on camera after her first bit of business of the day, but I had to go to work.

We made an arrangement for the following evening to meet Colin so that he could show us around the Gorman, where he was living. We said goodbye to Colin. I think the three of us, Deirdre, Ger and I, were shaken by what we had seen and heard that day. But even though a part of me was upset, inside me there was also a little man jumping up and down shouting, yippee! I knew I had good stuff in the can. Ger said it was interesting working with me. He had never filmed stuff like this before.

(Colleagues I have confided in since have told me not to worry about the little man inside shouting yippee. If ever you stop feeling that thrill when you've found something really awful, that means you've ceased to be a journalist and you're on your way to becoming a social worker instead.)

The next evening we waited, as arranged, at the Bridewell but there was no show from Colin or Ashley. The day after I had to think about what to do. We had only twenty-four hours left with the camera. I phoned Ger Cannon and asked him if he would be on for going directly to the Gorman and searching for interviewees, even without Colin to guide us. Ger said that was fine by him.

The Gorman is at the top of Morning Star Avenue, past the men's and women's hostels. The Gorman is the usual place a homeless person will go to if they can't get into one of the hostels.

The previous year, Deirdre and I went up to the Gorman on Good Friday morning after a woman, Eilish Lamour, was found dead there the day before. From the other homeless people at the Gorman I got the story of Eilish. She was in her early forties and spoke with a Northern accent. The day of her death, she was drunk and disruptive and was refused entry to the women's hostel. She wandered into the grounds of the Gorman and sat there on a bench where she drank cans for the rest of the day. Then she lay down to sleep. The next morning, a security man from a nearby building found her dead.

There were recent bruises on Eilish's body. The bruises were given to her by her boyfriend but it wasn't a beating that killed her. Eilish Lamour froze to death. Even though there was fine weather that week the nights could still be very cold, one of the homeless men told me. If you've drunk enough you don't feel the cold. I checked with the Met office. The night Eilish Lamour died the temperature was minus six. Later on that Good Friday, I told the story of Eilish Lamour on air to Rodney Rice.

Eilish Lamour died about two years after another homeless woman, Pauline Leonard, died in the same area in similar circumstances. Pauline was a Londoner whom I often met at Charles Street. I did a radio obituary on Pauline, too. In Easter of 1997, exactly two years after Eilish's death, I would do an obituary on yet another of Eilish's old drinking buddies found dead near the Gorman. That was Maxine Caffrey.

I knew that going into the Gorman with a camera was going to be different to all the times I had gone in there with a tape-recorder. I met Ger Cannon, my cameraman, at eight in the evening, as arranged. When we reached the old, crumbling gates of the grounds of the Gorman, we discussed what we would do if we ran into trouble. There would be lots of syringes in the Gorman, I had no doubt, so there was a danger of being mugged with one of these held to our throats. Dump the camera and run if you have to, I said to Ger. I'll do the explaining to RTE. Okay, said Ger, let's go to work.

On a bench outside the building a young couple with a baby in a buggy sat in the evening sun. They were poor and dirty-looking. I went up and introduced myself. I said I was expecting to meet Colin here. Has Colin been around? The young man answered in a strong Cork accent. Fuck off. I don't talk to cops.

Not for the first time, I was glad that I'm too small to be a policeman. At five-foot-nine I don't look like a cop. For too many of the people I meet, a stranger asking questions can only be a cop. At least my height, or lack of it, makes it easier for me to persuade people that I am who I say I am.

I showed the Corkman my RTE ID and pointed out Ger with the video camera. The Corkman was still suspicious. Then I remarked on his accent and told him I was from Cobh. The Corkman said he once worked as a fisherman in Cobh. I said that, in that case, he must know a certain fisherman based in the Holy Ground whom I sat next to in secondary school and made a radio programme with out in a boat in 1994, when I worked for RTE Radio Cork. The Corkman knew that fisherman very well.

The Corkman decided to trust me. Second last window on the second floor, he said. Colin's been in the Bridewell the last two days but he's back now.

Ger and I got as close to the building as the security fencing would allow us. I shouted Colin's name. Almost immediately Colin appeared at the window. Dressed only in his underpants, he stood in the window and did a sort of body-builder's pose. He shouted at Ger to get a shot of him. We'll be down in ten minutes, said Colin. Just give us a chance to get dressed.

Ger got shots of the Gorman while the sun was still up. The Gorman is a big old building. It has a neo-classical facade complete with a huge, crumbling, plaster emblem showing the coat-of-arms of some or other English monarch or noble. The Gorman is missing parts of its roof and most of its window panes. It's been out of service as a hospital for some years.

Colin and Ashley climbed out of a ground-floor window. Ashley was wearing a bright orange mini-dress. Colin, in his denims, was clean and scrubbed-looking as usual. We shook hands and I kissed Ashley on the cheek. Ger filmed all this. I'm sorry I didn't meet you yesterday, said Colin. I was in the Bridewell over a stupid thing but they let me out without charging me. Colin turned to the camera. Come in and see our home.

We got through a gap at one end of the security fencing, then in through the window. I had many times been in the grounds of the Gorman but I had never before gone into the building itself. The first room had the remains of tiles on the walls. It might have once been a bathroom. We went through to a darker room next door. This is the shooting-gallery, said Colin.

Our eyes adjusted, as did the camera, to the gloom. It was then that I saw that the ground was littered with syringes. Some had a spike still attached. People come here, said Ashley, with their children when they want to shoot up. It's not just people of the Gorman come here. It's a shooting-gallery for everybody in the Morning Star and Haven House as well.

I picked up one of the syringes and held it to the camera. Mind yourself Paddy, said Colin. He needn't have worried. I wouldn't have touched one with a spike on it.

There was incoherent shouting from another room. A woman's voice. I gathered she was shouting to Colin and Ashley. She was saying something about them owing her a turn-on. Colin was impatient. Don't mind Patricia. She's a nuisance.

I went to the room the shouting was coming from. Even though the ceiling and windows were missing, the room stank of alcohol. I will never forget what I saw in that room.

Patricia was on her hunkers against the wall. She was unusually fat for a junkie. I don't think she noticed me. She was too preoccupied with what she was trying to do to herself.

Patricia was skin-popping. When a junkie's vein is "blown", that is, collapsed from continuous abuse, it becomes impossible to inject in the usual way. Instead the junkie will stab the needle deep into some part of the flesh until the requisite amount of heroin has been delivered to the bloodstream. Patricia was holding the syringe in her right hand and was lunging at the soft flesh between the fingers of her left hand. Sometimes, in her drunkenness, she was missing her target but enough blows were landing to turn her hand into a mess of blood and torn flesh.

Colin led us away from Patricia and up the stairs. There are still signs on the walls and doors showing the matron's office, the names of wards and the like. How much this building has changed in its use since it was built. The matron that once had that office could never have imagined that her room would one day be used by homeless junkies. Nobody could ever have imagined the heroin disaster that would come to hit Dublin in the 1980s.

Mind the gaps in the floor, Paddy and Ger, said Colin. Ger filmed the death-trap holes in the corridor floor. I remember it was in the news a few years before when a homeless young man died in a fall in the Gorman. Now I could see how it happened. The drop from the first floor through to ground level is about thirty feet. In the darkness and perhaps under the influence of drink or drugs, it's difficult to see how anyone could survive a walk upstairs in the Gorman.

Mind the poos, said Ashley. Everywhere there were piles of human shit in various stages of hairy decay. Ashley and Colin showed us makeshift beds in the various rooms off the corridor. These rooms will be full later, they said.

Colin and Ashley brought us into their room. There was a sheet hung up as a door. Inside the room it was brighter than in the corridor, making the camera's job easier. There was a mattress in one corner and a basin and some toiletries in another. No other furniture. There was rubbish and debris piled at one wall. Colin pointed out the droppings of mice or maybe rats.

We sat on the mattress for a three-shot for camera. Ashley, as ever, was mild-mannered and talkative. For the first time since I had met her a few days before, it occurred to me that Ashley was a beautiful woman. Up until now I had only seen the illness of drug addiction. Now I was looking past that and I could see what a good-looking woman she was, or could be, if she could only get off drugs.

Colin sounded anxious in the interview, desperate that the world should understand what he had to say. He interrupted Ashley a lot, even when my questions were directed at her rather than at him. Why don't Dublin Corporation give us a chance, Paddy? Why won't they give us a place together?

Do you have rent arrears, Colin?

Seven hundred pound, but I can't pay that until I get off drugs. And we want to get married, Paddy. See Ashley's engagement ring? Are you getting that on the camera, Ger? Me and her love each other.

Colin searched for his spoon but couldn't find it so he improvised. He found a Coke can then tore the bottom off it with his bare hands. He fashioned the ripped metal sides into a handle then held what was the concave bottom of the can upside down to turn it into a substitute for a spoon. Ashley opened her handbag and took out a small, white package. This is citric powder, said Colin. It cleans the heroin. I noticed that Ashley had condoms and paper hankies in her handbag. They're two items that all prostitutes carry.

Colin took a packet from the breast pocket of his jacket and held it up to the camera. Are you getting this, Ger? This is enough heroin for just one turn-on but I'm giving it to Ashley cos I love her.

Colin mixed the citric, heroin and water in the upturned Coke can bottom. He held it over his cigarette lighter until the mixture boiled. He took the filter out of a cigarette, spread it out flat and dipped it into the mixture. (I don't know what purpose the filter serves.) He pressed the syringe against the filter and drew the mixture up into the barrel. He attached the spike while Ashley wrapped a strap around her upper arm and pumped her lower arm to get a vein up.

Colin took his lover's arm and pressed the needle into a vein. Ashley began to cry. Don't do it there, Colin. The vein's blown.

It's not blown, said Colin. Stay still. You'll be all right in a moment.

It's blown, Colin. It's fucking blown.

I whispered to Ger to get the camera off Ashley's arm and onto her face.

Colin was firm with Ashley. He ignored her crying and forced the needle obliquely into her vein. He drew back the plunger and the barrel of the syringe filled with Ashley's blood.

I'm going to give it to you now, love. You'll be all right.

Colin pushed the plunger. The heroin-rich blood surged into Ashley's arm.

The effect on Ashley was immediate. Her face lost its look of pain and took on a look of relief. She began to breathe deeply.

Moments later she looked at Colin with love in her eyes. That's good, she said, and gave a small chuckle.

Ashley spoke to the camera. She was calm and coherent. That's me sorted now, until the next time. Heroin makes you feel good. You forget about your problems for awhile.

For awhile.

Searching for Ashley: Grangegorman; the Whores of Benburb Street; Eastern Health Board office, Charles Street; St Michael's Estate, Inchicore;
November 1996

It was four months since I had met Ashley. I put my completed video into the hands of various television producers in RTE and hoped that someone would take up my programme proposal. In the meantime, I knew from the time I met Ashley that I had somebody worth broadcasting and whereas I knew that my television idea might or might not ever happen, I still had my radio programme of which I was the boss. It was just a matter of finding Ashley again.

I went to the Gorman early one morning and waited for the people sleeping there to come out. I brought cigarettes and when the first people emerged, I lit up and let the cigarette dangle from my fingers. I don't smoke but I knew smoking would be a good idea this morning.

Two young men and a teenage girl came out. Watching them emerging from the Gorman, it reminded me of the news footage you see of Bosnia, with people emerging from ruined, bomb-ravaged buildings. Through the security fencing, I called out to them and told them who I was and who I was looking for. The men were Dubliners. They were unfriendly. Are you the fellah from the telly? You paid Ashley and Colin a lot of money and then they got a flat because of you. They told you a whole load of bullshit. Now put us on the telly and pay us for it. Or else fuck off.

I told them that no television programme was broadcast and that I had never paid Colin or Ashley anything. The two men didn't believe me. You're bullshit, they said. And Ashley is bullshit. She says she was bleedin' raped. How is it she's the only bleedin' one on Benburb Street always gets raped? She's a gee-bag. She deserved it.

I kept nodding along with these aggressive bastards. I was on their territory at the Gorman. I wasn't going to cross them. Then the teenager spoke. She was a Londoner. Could you spare us a cigarette please, mate?

My cigarette bait had worked. I passed cigarettes to the three of them. I said to them that I believed that Benburb Street was a dangerous place to work and that I was willing to take Ashley's word for it when she said she was attacked. The Londoner spoke again, her voice timid and quiet next to the ranting of the Dubliners. I'm a prostitute too, she said. First at King's Cross in London and now here in Dublin. She met the two Dubliners through sleeping rough at King's Cross. Now, all junkies together, they were in Dublin.

The Londoner would be a good person to talk to, I could tell. But there was no point in trying to talk when her two loud-mouthed friends were with her. Someday, maybe, I would get to speak to her on her own. I said goodbye to the three young people and told them I would see them again some time, maybe to make a radio programme.

Later that evening, I went to Benburb Street. Chances were that Ashley still worked there. I arrived around seven and sat in the car. It was freezing. Every now and again I turned on the car's engine just to warm up for awhile. The women eyed me, wondering if I was a customer. I realised, now, that Benburb Street had changed in the last few years. I remembered it as a place of rough-looking, alcoholic, middle-aged women but now it was full of young women, probably all of them junkies. I guess that when the young junkies moved in, the older women didn't stand a chance.

A woman was standing at the corner of the road that leads up to Arbour Hill. She wore a ludicrous short skirt in the freezing cold. It was Tina. The same woman I had seen in the summer evening four months before. After a while Tina walked towards my car. She gave me a big smile as she came to the passenger-side door and got me to roll down the window. Are you doing business?

I told Tina I was waiting for Ashley. I'm a reporter, I said, and Ashley knows a lot about services for drug addicts in this city and she's helping me with my research. (I didn't tell Tina that I wanted to talk to Ashley about prostitution. I wasn't sure how the other Benburb Street women might react to Ashley talking to a journalist about that.)

Ah, you're a reporter, said Tina, still smiling. Asho won't be around today. She goes to see her kids on a Tuesday. I'm a junkie too. The drugs is terrible, isn't it? I have to do this for my habit. I charge forty pounds for sex. For twenty I'll help you do it to yourself and let you see me mary. Are you doing business?

I had been considering asking Tina if she wanted to do an interview but then I realised that what I had said about being a reporter seemed to have passed her by. To Tina, I was a man sitting in a good car and I was either doing business or I was not. No, Tina. I'm not doing business. If you see Ashley please tell her I'm looking for her.

Later that evening, I told Deirdre about Tina. Deirdre said I had to look at it from Tina's point of view. Tina was the one standing around having the mary frozen off her as she listened to all sorts of nonsense from the men she met. Ashley had told us about one of her regulars at Benburb Street who said he was a reporter. Now Tina was faced with me. Another fellow who says he's a reporter. So Tina smiled and nodded along with what I was saying but there came a point when she needed to know if I was doing business or not.

The next morning, in my search for Ashley, I tried the Eastern Health Board office at Charles Street. It's where homeless people go for money or for vouchers for a hostel. It's near the Four Courts. The security man there, who knows me over the years, said he hadn't seen Colin and Ashley for some time. He thought they might have got a flat somewhere.

That was hard for me to make sense of. Colin and Ashley had rent arrears. The Corporation gives people plenty of chances before evicting them but once you're evicted, the Corpo won't re-house you unless you make some arrangement for paying off the arrears. So how could Colin and Ashley have got a corporation flat? Surely they hadn't given up heroin, cleared their arrears and applied for a place? That was hard to imagine. I decided I would stick around Charles Street awhile more with my tape-recorder and meet more people and ask more questions. Even if I didn't find Ashley, I knew I would pick up good material for broadcast.

Mornings at Charles Street are for the women and children and also for the refugees from Romania, parts of Africa and other places. Up until a few years ago, everybody had to queue here together in the afternoons. I often highlighted this on my radio programme. I never said anything specific about this. Just interviewed the women with kids, the junkies, the winos and the psychotics all in the same queue and the point made itself. Now things had improved slightly with this segregation of the homeless by sex. Women in the mornings and men in the afternoons.

A young man and two young women came out. I recognised two of them as a brother and sister whom I had interviewed before. They were junkies. Their mother and step-father were among seven people who drowned when their car went into Dublin's Grand Canal one night a few years earlier.

After their parents' death, the brother and sister told me, they were cared for by their grandmother who couldn't cope with them as unruly teenagers. They blamed their mother's death for their turning to drugs. That's not an explanation I would readily accept. After all, there are plenty of junkies whose mothers are alive and well, but I accept that the canal tragedy did help to further stack the odds against two young people who were already disadvantaged.

I was pleased to see that brother and sister again. I was glad they were still alive and sad they were still addicts. I was moved, as ever, by their closeness and loyalty to each other. The man shook my hand and spoke to his friend. He's all right, he said of me.

The man was small and scrawny. He spoke with the slow, groaning voice that's common among addicts and which, I learned since, shows that a person has injected heroin within the last hour or so.

What were you doing in Charles Street, I asked? Are you homeless?

They told me they had recently been thrown out of their place in Summerhill. Not by the Corporation but by the "vijoes", that is, the vigilantes. Their flat was marched on and the tenant, their friend, was told to put them out or she would herself be put out. It ended up with the three of them being made homeless. It was all on the telly.

I had seen that eviction on the news. It was one of many evictions going on around that time. And where were they expected to go? In reply the young man explained, succinctly, the attitude of the non-drug-using public to junkies such as himself. Nobody gives a bollocks where we go so long as we're not near them.

And were they dealing drugs? They accused us of drug-dealing but if we were dealing drugs we wouldn't be dressed like this.

I questioned them a bit further about this. After all, I suggested, addicts often deal drugs. They told the truth without any more prompting. They dealt heroin in the past. In return, their supplier allowed them every tenth deal free.

Once again, I saw that the distinction between addict and dealer isn't as clear-cut as is sometimes thought. "Pushers out" is just a bit of rhetoric. It really means "Addicts out". If you get addicts in your housing estate, you will get drugs being dealt. The true drug barons don't live in local authority estates. It is junkies such as that brother and sister who will bring drugs into the area and cause drugs to be available to your children.

A few weeks earlier I had been in court to see a family put out by the Corporation for "estate management reasons" which meant drug dealing. In court, Mrs Clifford admitted that her three sons were dealing drugs from her house in Tallaght. But, she said, the three of them were gone now. One was in England, one in prison and one she knew not where. Only her daughter and grandchild lived with her now and the drug-dealing had ended.

Mrs Clifford's twenty-four-year-old daughter, Sharon, told the court she had a drug habit but she denied dealing drugs.

Sharon said that, like her mother, she and her baby would have nowhere to go if she was evicted. Counsel for the Cliffords gave evidence that there were no convictions for drug dealing against either of the women facing eviction.

The judge explained to the court that Dublin Corporation, which was seeking to evict the Cliffords, didn't have to deal with what he called the merits of the case. Perhaps it should matter, said the judge, that the family, if evicted, would have nowhere to go, but in law, he said, it didn't matter. He gave the Corporation possession of the house at a date three weeks from the day of the hearing.

The anti-drugs activists from Tallaght, who were in the court, were pleased with the result. They told me they had tried to get Mrs Clifford a house out of their area but that she wouldn't co-operate. Now there was one less house in Tallaght in which their children might be drawn into drug use. When I asked where the Cliffords would go nobody was too concerned. There are hostels in Dublin, they said, or they could go to England.

So eviction from their homes and, if possible, from their country, was now the order of the day for dealing with junkies. The vigilantes were doing it and the local authorities were doing it. Eviction is easy. After that, some junkies go to England. Others stay in Dublin where they sleep rough in the Gorman, the Phoenix Park, or the loading bays of shopping centres. Nobody gives a bollocks where we go so long as we're not near them.

You fucking black bastard. You fucking whoremaster. What are you fucking looking at?

The entrance for refugees at Charles Street is at the side of the building. The woman shouting abuse at one of the blacks looked like a prostitute and therefore, I thought, she might know Ashley. She looked about eighteen years old. She was skinny and sick-looking and had bad acne. A junkie.

It was her pants that were most noticeable. She wore a cut-off pair of faded blue jeans that were stuck up tight between her buttocks and cut high and raggedly to either side, showing off most of the cheeks of her bottom. She was small and tottered along on a pair of platform sandals.

This youngster was pleased to talk to me. There's no place for us cos we're Irish but if you have a black face you get fucking everything. I'm just after being refused a place in the hostel.

She told me about her drug addiction and about having been threw ou' o' me gaff by her mum and dad. She had repeated convictions for shoplifting and expected to be soon sent to Mountjoy. I didn't ask her about her ludicrous clothing in November. We didn't get around to that because when I asked about Ashley, she knew all about her.

Asho and me are great friends. She's squatting in Inchicore. St Michael's Estate.

Good. After just a few days searching, I had a good lead on where to find Ashley. I would go to St Michael's the next morning.

I should have guessed that Ashley and Colin were squatting. That's how they got a place without clearing their arrears. The blocks of flats in St Michael's have plenty of empty flats that could be broken into. As well as that, St Michael's, I had heard, had been left alone by the vigilantes. It would have been hard for the like of Colin and Ashley to get into most places but St Michael's was still open to them because the vijoes had no hold over the place.

St Michael's would not be natural vijoe territory. Most working-class areas of Dublin have extended family and neighbourhood links that make it hard for anybody to hide their wrongdoings, drug dealing or whatever, from the rest of the community. A junkie who is thrown out of one area will find it hard to get in anywhere else because his reputation will precede him. Hence, Concerned Parents Against Drugs in the 1980s and their successors in the 1990s were able to use family and neighbourhood links to keep junkies and dealers on the run.

But St Michael's is different. There is no extended family or neighbourhood structure there. Even at the height of the housing shortage of the previous few years, a housing applicant was always likely to get an offer of St Michael's because nobody wanted to live there and people were always moving out. Like Ballymun, St Michael's is full of single mothers and their transient boyfriends. There is nothing that you could call a local community in St Michael's. So the vijoes had left St Michael's alone, causing a general shift of the drug problem in the south inner city away from Dolphin's Barn and into Inchicore.

I had been in St Michael's Estate many times before. I made a programme there in the summer of 1991. The sewage had backed up through the toilets and flooded out a number of flats and there were pools of sewage coming up from the drains outside. I went around talking to residents. It was easy to get them to talk about the sewage problem in particular and after that, about the estate in general and the circumstances that led them to accept flats here. The programme was debated at a subsequent meeting of Dublin Corporation. I enjoyed making that programme.

Now I was back here looking for Ashley and Colin. It was mid-morning. I made straight for Block Eight, the one most likely to be squatted in. I asked a woman downstairs about Colin and Ashley and she told me which floor to go to. I was in the right place. I never trust the lifts so I took the stairs.

There's a smell of rubbish and piss on every landing. Graffiti everywhere. Some abandoned flats have steel doors to stop squatters. The Corporation theory is that they will eventually refurbish these flats and let them out for rent.

On the fifth floor there was graffiti urging people not to leave "workses", that is, syringes, lying around where children might pick them up. I could see no syringes but I found pieces of silver paper with scorch marks and empty plastic sterile water containers from the needle exchange at Pearse Street. Clearly, junkies were using the landings.

I reached the door that I was told was Ashley and Colin's. I knocked. A man's shout came from inside. Fuck off.

I knocked again. Colin, is that you?

The door opened. It was Colin and he was angry. Who are you? What do you want?

Then he remembered me. Colin took me in his arms and hugged me. Paddy, come in. We were only talking about you. Sorry for shouting. I thought you were someone come looking for a turn-on. Ashley, we have a friend here.

Ashley came out to the corridor. Her hair was tied back and she looked thinner than ever. Her skin was taut against her skull as she beamed a smile at me. She was small in her bare feet. I saw that her arms were smeared in blood as she stretched them out to embrace me. She hugged my neck and patted my back and kissed me. Her eyes showed delight at seeing me. The level of Colin and Ashley's warmth towards me is something I have never quite understood.

They brought me in. There was a third person in the front room. He was hunched over by the telly with one shoe and sock off. This is Anto, said Colin. Anto nodded at me vaguely and turned back to whatever he was doing with his foot.

I'll make you a cup of tea in a moment, Paddy, said

Ashley. You caught us at a bad moment. We were just having a turn-on.

There was blood everywhere. It was Ashley's blood. She was having difficulty getting a vein up so a lot of attempts had already been made on her arm that morning and her arm was showing the damage.

I saw again the procedure I had seen some months before in the Gorman as Colin dealt deftly with the heroin, the citric, the water, his spoon and lighter, the cigarette filter then his tourniquet and syringe. Colin injected himself first then saw to Ashley. Give us your works there Ashley, said Colin. They had three separate syringes. Anto still had his back to me. I realised he was injecting himself in the foot.

Colin took Ashley's arm and pushed the needle in. She began to cry. Fuck you, you're on a bone. The fucking citric is burning me. It's burning me, Colin.

Moments later she stopped crying and started complaining. I didn't get any hit out of that. You didn't put enough in.

Colin's eyes were gone back in his head and he answered Ashley in a deep, throaty groan. I didn't get any hit either, he said. This stuff is no good.

Ashley was comtemptuous. She looked at me for support. Do you hear the voice on him, Paddy? And he says he didn't get a hit!

For the first time I realised that the groaning voice that I often heard before from junkies is a sign that the person has just turned on. The hit was working for Colin but not for Ashley.

Ashley got up to go to the bedroom for more gear. The syringe was still stuck in her arm and she held it loosely as she walked about the flat. It was routine for Ashley to go around with a works hanging out of her. Her blood was smeared everywhere now. On her arms, her blouse, on the table and chairs and on my coat. Then she was back and the citric and heroin cooking began again. Colin made another attempt at her arm. This time Ashley was satisfied.

Anto was finished turning on, too. Anto was fresh-faced and in his early twenties. He looked healthy and had a gentle Dublin accent. I wouldn't have guessed that he was a junkie. He wouldn't have seemed out of place serving you in a bank or in a shop. Anto apologized for having his back turned on me while he was seeing to his foot. He didn't mean to be rude.

Ashley made tea. I barely touched it. I know I can't get Aids from a teacup, even if any of the three people I was with had that disease, but Hepatitis spreads much more easily. I poured most of the tea down the sink when they weren't looking.

Colin had gone now into oblivion, his eyes rolling back in his head. Anto and Ashley would get a chance to talk. Anto wanted to impress me. He had good jobs in the past, he said. Now he was getting off drugs and would get back to working and earning money. Anto spoke earnestly to my microphone about how drugs had ruined his life and how he felt more help was needed for people like himself. The Merchants Quay Project were helping him. He was to see a counsellor the following Friday with a view to getting onto a detoxification course.

I believed Anto. Not only did I believe that he meant what he said about wanting to get off gear, I also believed that he was serious about taking steps to make that wish come true. Good for you, Anto. I hope you succeed.

Of course, I shouldn't have believed any of it. Anto, I would find out soon enough, was another one who would never take responsibility for himself. I met him some months later and asked him how the meeting went with his

counsellor. He had missed it. He was "sick", that is, in need
of a turn-on that morning and he decided there was no point
seeing the counsellor when he was sick. He needed to get
sorted first, then he would be able to see his counsellor
another day and see about getting a detox. Until then, Anto
would stay on drugs. Typical junkie.

Anto said he was lucky to have his own works. In the last
few weeks, the police had been confiscating workses from
the junkies all around Dolphin's Barn. They had a big white
bucket in the back of the garda van and they were throwing
all the workses in that. It's because of all the attacks with
syringes, said Anto. I told Anto that it was on the news that
morning that a man escaped from a prison van on the Naas
Road when he produced a syringe and held it to the throat of
a prison officer. Is that right?, said Anto. Now the police will
really go mad. If you take away clean workses people are
going to share a dirty works and you'll get more virus.

Ashley said she was going to Benburb Street in the
afternoon. Colin couldn't come with her any more, she said,
because he had warrants and he couldn't risk being seen by
the police. Now, she tries to do all regulars. Her deaf and
dumb fellow was due tonight. They do it in the back of his
van. I asked if I could join Ashley later and she said yes.

I took out a videotape from my coat. It was the completed
version of the work I had done with them four months
before. Please look at it, I said, if you can get to see it
somewhere, and tell me what you think. I'll see you later,
Ashley.

Ashley turned up that afternoon at Benburb Street, as she
said she would. I was parked at the lower end of the street
on the left along with the usual line of parked trucks. There
was one woman standing across the road from me outside the
pub. I spotted Ashley in the distance in my wing mirror,

walking alongside the high wall of Collins's Barracks. I wasn't sure at first if it was she. Her hair was down and she was in her working clothes. Shiny silver pants and top. It was hard to imagine her as the blood-smeared, drug-starved junkie I had seen crying in pain that morning.

Ashley gave me a big smile as she came near. I was delighted to see her, too. During the four months since I had first met Ashley outside the Bridewell, I had been messing about with an attempted television programme, trying to find a way of getting a terrific interviewee on air. Now, at last, I was working for radio again. I'm a radio producer. That means I'm the boss of my own show and I decide what goes on air. I had my interviewee to myself and I knew I was getting a good programme for broadcast the following Saturday.

Ashley sat next to me in my car and I took out my tape recorder and microphone.

Okay, we're here at Benburb Street. It's five in the evening and you're about to go to work. What time will you work until today?

Until about eleven tonight. It all depends on the business. I'll get into about four cars and when I have eighty pounds that's enough. You'd wait maybe an hour for your first car and then sometimes you might be only ten minutes. Well, Thursday or Friday night you're only waiting ten minutes anyway cos it's pay day for them. Sunday night is no good cos they bring their wives to the pubs. You learn what nights to come out.

You've learned a lot about this job.

I have. It'll be a year Christmas since I came here first. Two days before Christmas it was. Like I know now what to wear. I won't be waiting too long tonight to get picked up cos, well, I've wore all different clothes down here and the suit I have on me now . . . jees . . . I wore it down last night and it was brilliant. I was jumping in and out of cars all night. They're called hipsters. And the top is to match. There's a zip at the top of it and it's pulled down and you can see me cleavage and you can see me belly. It's kind of a belly-top. So it's showing off me bum and showing off me figure. (Ashley was laughing now.) And that works especially with me zip pulled down and they want to know how big are they and have you got big . . . nibbles. And have you got hair down there and things like that they ask you and I tell them they're going to have to pay to find out and some of them do and some of them just walk off.

Some men are mad like. They just keep driving around looking at the girls. I seen a fellow and he doing it to himself as he's driving around looking at us. You can get weirdos. Some of them wants to put bottles up you, ones that wants to put bananas up you. You get mad ones. They have mad kinks they have. You get ones that wants to whip you. I know one fellow was giving me a hundred pound one night for . . . to go up . . . anal, is that what you say? (Ashley seemed embarrassed here, as much, I think, by her uncertainty about the right anatomical words as by what it was she was talking about.) You get ones that wants to whip you. I know one fellah he just comes to talk cos he was whipped out in the Middle East. He was the reporter I told you about before, Paddy.

Ashley told me about the reporter who was one of her regulars at Benburb Street. You see, Paddy, he was out in Arabia and he was whipped there for having drink on him and all the women watched him being whipped cos the women whip men in those countries and he never got over it and now he has to come here to talk about it cos he needs to talk about it.

213

I nodded along with this story without challenging it. It didn't occur to Ashley that what she had heard from her supposed reporter was nothing more than a male, masturbatory fantasy. I could see it all. This guy gets his jollies telling Ashley the story largely because she believes it. A more experienced prostitute or, I guess, any woman more experienced in the ways of men, would recognise the whipping story for the nonsense that it was. Still, I suppose the guy was paying Ashley to listen to him and as long as it stayed at fantasy level no harm would come to her. No need to tell Ashley that her famous reporter was just a wanker.

This reporter, Ashley. Did he ever do more than just talk about whipping?

You know the way, Paddy, he was with a film crew in Arabia and he made a video of the whipping and he was giving me a hundred pounds one night to go back to his place and he wanted to whip me and all this and handcuff me and I said no. I was too frightened of going back to his house.

I don't want to keep you too long here because I know you need to go to work but tell me about the men you meet.

Most of them are married men. Like it's usually about five, six in the evening and they want their bit before they come home from work cos they know they're not going to get it off their wives. I mean some of them say their wife's only after having a kid or their wife has a bad back. They have all excuses.

You have marks and cysts on your arms from the needle . . .

Loads.

Do the men not realise that when you undress for them?

No. Like, I have an abscess on me hand where Colin went into me bone this morning. Do you see that? I can hardly move that, it's so sore. The men are only after the one thing.

214

Most of them know that you're on drugs. Like I always make up a story that I'm doing it for something else, like I'm doing it for me kids' books, but most of them know and some of them do feel sorry for you and they give me another twenty quid when they're getting out the car. Like that's a bonus and you can go home early. Like one night a fellow brought me out to Dollymount and I had a lump in me throat cos I was talking about me children and he brought me for a drink and I was going home and he says here, and he gave me a hundred pound.

Tell me about your regulars.

I think all the girls have regulars. It's great when you get into a car with a regular cos you know you're not going to be attacked, you know you're not going to get raped, you know you're not going to get robbed. It's great when you see somebody you know . . . there's two coppers now.

Two uniformed police approached. I got ready with my explanation. They glanced in at us but walked by without stopping.

You were arrested once?

Yeah. They were after telling me to go home but I hadn't made a penny so there was no way I was going home. I had a warrant that time so I ended up in Mountjoy for five days. Then they let me go on my own bail but I didn't turn up in court then after that cos I was too embarrassed. I don't want them all in court to see me and know what I was up for. There's still a warrant now. They can pick you up any time. They bring you to the night court at ten o'clock and then they can remand you in custody. I've a few charges. I'm up again in February.

I took a note of the date and time of Ashley's next Bridewell appearance.

How did you start on heroin?

Two years ago I got a flat in Fatima and drugs was everywhere and I was on Valium six years since my mother died and there was this man, a big drug baron, he's in prison now and he asked me to go over to . . . across the seas, I'll say, and he gave me four hundred pounds to bring drugs back over to this country. And this time I wasn't on drugs and, Jesus Christ, four hundred pounds was good money and I did it and I had the kids at the time and, you know, I was just thinking of the four hundred pound and I came back and I got the money and gave him his drugs. And he was putting drugs on the tinfoil for me and I wasn't paying for them and they made me feel good and that life was great, that I hadn't got a problem in the world. Then all of a sudden he stopped giving me the drugs then I had to start paying for them. And he was a completely different person then. And he threw the drugs into me to do another trip for him but I started getting afraid and I wouldn't do it for him and that's when he started making me pay for the drugs. And then I couldn't afford me habit and I was wakening up, pains in me back, pains in me legs, I was getting sick and just kept going to the toilet and I was in bits and I was going out and getting drugs. In the beginning I didn't believe that I was strung out. I said to myself I'm not strung out, it's flu I have. But I was strung out. As soon as I stuck a needle into me arm the pains was gone. I knew then I was strung out.

Tell me about your heroin habit now.

Well, I had two this morning when I got up. Then I collected me labour, that's sixty pound. Then got another two. Then I got four before I came out. Two for him and two for me cos I support his habit too cos I don't want him going out robbing and getting locked up. Before I came here I used to do shops for my habit but now the shops all know me. I'm barred from half the shops in Dublin. But I hate this. I hate doing this. I feel dirty. I blame myself for letting men do this to me. Like it's very hard to get off heroin especially when you know you can get the money here.

Ashley sounded now like my old friends, Frances and Rose, who had since died. I remember Frances saying she would always spend her money on heroin when she knew she could make it up again at Benburb Street. Too bloody easy, said Frances. I wondered how long Ashley would live if she didn't get off heroin.

Can you get heroin easily?

It's very easy where we are now cos it's in the flat above me and it's in the flat next door and if we don't have it we go to them or if they don't have it they come to us. But I want to get off heroin now. Me court case is coming up in December and I'm looking for the kids and if I don't get them back you'll read about me cos– I'd say he's a punter, that car in front of me.

Okay, Ashley, I won't keep you from your work any more . . .

Yeah, he's a punter. Jenny's getting in with him . . . me arm is killing me, it is, where he went into the bone this morning. Listen, God Bless. Mind yourself, Paddy.

Ashley kissed me and got out to cross the road. A man approached her on foot. He wasn't like the other fat cats in their cars. He was scruffy and in his mid-twenties. Ashley looked pleased at whatever he said and she gave him a smile. Then she came back to me and knocked on my car window. She had forgotten her umbrella. I handed it out to her. She told me she had just got a lane job. That's twenty quid to start with. God Bless, Paddy.

I watched Ashley re-join her customer. It was dark now. They walked up the long hill of Benburb Street together.

led the man into a lane and was gone from my

The Night Train, Pearse Street, Dublin;
January, 1997

Ashley had told me about the night train and I decided it was
something I would explore. The night train isn't a train of any
sort, nor is it anything even mobile. I don't know how it got
the name. The night train is the night time clinic for drug
addicts at Trinity Court, Pearse Street, in Dublin.

As with the daytime clinic, addicts go to the night clinic to
get their methadone maintenance or "phye" (physeptome),
which helps to keep their craving for heroin at bay. But the
night service is different to the day service in one important
respect. In the daytime clinic, an addict has to provide urine
samples to prove that he has been abstaining from taking
heroin or any other drugs. If he is found to have "dirty urine",
he will be denied his methadone. At the night train, no urine
sample is asked for. Rather, the addict is given his methadone
and maybe also clean needles and condoms. It is fully
expected that the addict is going to continue taking drugs. The
prescribed methadone, in this case, is not expected to detox
him but simply to stabilise his habit and prevent him from
becoming ill and desperate for drugs. It's a damage limitation
exercise. The night train can be regarded as an admission of
failure, by addict and clinic alike, to wean the addict off drugs.

I was many times before outside the Pearse Street clinic
but this was my first time tackling the night train. It was about
six in the evening and it was already dark. The addicts were
there, same as during the daytime, standing around the
modern, red-brick building of Trinity Court or sitting on the

steps of the houses nearby. Some of those houses are derelict. Others contain offices or businesses and I'm sure the tenants are none too happy to have the addicts hanging around.

Tonight there was a crowd of about forty young men and women. They were a noisy lot. A lot of raised voices and tension. Fook this and you fook off, in the strong, exaggerated-sounding Dublin accent that addicts have. Why all the shouting? The daytime addicts are generally calmer. Before the evening was over, I would understand better what all the anxiety was about.

I scanned the crowd for familiar faces. If there was even one person I knew that would help to give me an in. I could find no one. I have got to know plenty of junkies here at Pearse Street over the years but they die. Every couple of years, I have to make new contacts among drug addicts. Tonight, I was approaching these people anew once again.

I sat on the steps next to a group of them. I had my tape-recorder and microphone on my lap. After a few moments, I got their attention. Excuse me, folks, I'm doing some work here for RTE Radio. I'm looking to speak to anyone who wants to tell me about the service that's available here for drug addicts.

I was surrounded and quickly overwhelmed by hopeful interviewees. They were all screaming at me at once and then screaming at each other to shut up and give each other a chance to talk. In the dark, their faces look even more cadaverous than they normally do. They have rotten teeth, skin taut against the cheekbones, eyes deep in skull-like sockets. These people are very ill. Some of them are in late Aids.

I was as polite as I could be to everybody. This took patience. Some people, when they got their chance on the microphone, went into monologues about how they were cut

219

off from the day clinic and got fooked onto the night train. It surprised me how many people seemed wounded about being put on the night train. These people said they still wanted to get off drugs. They wanted just one more detox, and then one more after that. Others were so anxious to talk to me that they kept interrupting. When I would quieten them, some of them grew angry. There's no point talking to him, one shouted as he stormed away. He doesn't want to fooking know.

I was watching and listening for the kind of interviewees I wanted. It's my belief that heroin addicts, like alcoholics, are generally people of above-average intelligence. I've got to know and like a lot of them over the years and some of my best interviews have come from here at Pearse Street. If I could just calm people down, tell them I would get around to everybody who wanted to talk to me, which I would, then I would get good material here tonight.

Why are you here at the night train?

Two young women answered. We got fooked off the day clinic cos they said we gave dirty urines but my urines was spotless but I couldn't give a urine with somebody watching me. It's very embarrassing to go to the toilet with somebody watching you and a mirror behind you but because I couldn't go to the toilet they classed that as a dirty urine.

I understood this story. Addicts sometimes give "false urines", that is, somebody else's urine, in an attempt to beat the urine test. I guess they use little bottles hidden in their pants, or something like that. The result has been that some addicts are asked to pee while under close observation.

So are you getting methadone from the clinic tonight?

We're not going to the clinic.

What do you mean?

We're here for phye, valium, rollies or whatever's going.

A man interrupted. I'm here since two o'clock and there's no bleedin' phye around. I have some rollies here if you want some.

He sold them two pills for a pound each. They thanked him earnestly. Rollies are Rhohipnol, a type of sleeping pill that addicts use to keep their sickness at bay and help them through the night.

I was beginning to understand, now, what was going on. The prescription methadone coming out of Trinity Court was only a small part of what attracted people to this place. The two women were here, like most of the others, not to attend the clinic but to see what was for sale on the street. There's no heroin here but Pearse Street is the place where prescription drugs, including methadone, are bought and sold. I had seen this going on outside the day clinic but the night train attracts the most desperate and sick of Dublin's drug addicts. The anxiety and tension here were all to do with the desperate need these people had for drugs.

Hello, Paddy. It was somebody I knew. Ammo, it's good to see you. I heard you were dead.

I remember when I first met Ammo, six years before, outside Mountjoy Prison, I didn't know for several minutes if I was talking to a man or a woman. Ammo was still dressed much the same tonight. A combat jacket and heavy boots and a close-cropped, military-style haircut. I worked out Ammo's sex when I got the story about the punishment cell in Mountjoy. Why were you put in solitary? Cos a girl came in and she was crying cos it was her first time in prison so I went to kiss her because she was upset and they said I was making a pass at her and put me in solitary. I wasn't making a pass at her because I wouldn't have done anything to upset her.

I had met Ammo once before here at Pearse Street, too. I remember, for tape, she gave me a running commentary on

221

what was going on around us. When two old men had come along, Ammo said to me, you'd never think they were dealing drugs, would you Paddy? I was astonished. No Ammo, I would not. It turned out they were OAPs who got prescription valium or sleeping pills or whatever which they then brought to Pearse Street to sell to the addicts. After the sale, they would drink the proceeds. I remember I looked at those old men with approval. I mean, who wants anti-depressants and shite like that if you can swap them for the money for a few pints?

And I remember later that day, I gave Ammo a lift home. She was wearing an Eric Cantona jersey and, when she found some of my son's Manchester United magazines in the car, she insisted on getting some of her own fan club paraphernalia from her home for me to bring home to my son. She opened up one magazine and found a picture of Ryan Giggs with his girlfriend. Would you fancy her, Paddy? She's lovely, Ammo. Would you fancy her? Ammo smiled in reply. She seemed pleased that I had acknowledged something that we had never spoken openly about before. Ammo is bisexual.

Now, tonight, at the night train, I was surprised to see that Ammo was still alive. She had been HIV-positive for at least six years now. Tonight she was cheerful and friendly like she always was but she didn't look well. She had a cyst the size of a grape on the back of her left hand, forcing her fingers into a claw. Her skin had deteriorated and was showing the sores and redness that seem to go with late Aids. I've been through a lot, Paddy. I was living with a girl in Kilburn, but I came back. When I was away, a lot of people heard the rumour I was dead. I read your book. When you write your next one I want you to write about me. I will, Ammo, I said, but, I thought to myself, I wonder if you'll still be alive to see it published?

A row broke out among the addicts. It was two women. She said I took her fooking phye. I never fooking touched ah.

Other women jumped in, screaming. They were held back from each other. I had never seen junkies act so aggressively before. This place was a nightmare.

A woman walked up to me. Am I getting paid if I talk to you? No. I'm sorry, you're not. Well that's a disgrace. She stormed off.

Two plainclothes policemen were making no attempt to appear inconspicuous. They were big, fit, healthy-looking men. They kept an eye on proceedings but didn't intervene. I don't know if the street sale of prescription drugs, which was what was going on here, is or isn't illegal. Then the two cops approached a man they may have been waiting for and took him away. He started shouting at me as he was escorted past me in the direction of Pearse Street Garda Station. They didn't show me any ID. Put that on your radio programme. I waved an acknowledgment to him. I didn't think he needed to worry whether they were genuine cops. Two big footballers among the scrawny Dublin junkies. They were cops.

A man aged about forty-five with a Belfast accent spoke to me. He showed me the syringe he had just got from the clinic. That's for me. That way I can stay clean. I was surprised to meet someone with that accent and of that age. He told me he was living in Dublin for many years. I mentioned the names of other junkies of his generation, now all dead, and he was pleased to talk about them. There was very few of us junkies in those days, he said, and we always looked after each other. It's different now.

He went away, telling me the name of the nearby fast food restaurant outside whose doors he was about to score. I understood what he meant about things being different now. He was from the hippy generation, from a different social and cultural background to the other junkies here. Now, his friends all dead, he was stuck on the night train.

A young woman came up to me. She smiled at me and hugged me. Is that Paddy? She had a distinctive Wicklow accent. I remembered her from the time I interviewed her in her home in Bray. She was evicted from her local authority house there because of drugs. Originally, Bray UDC said it would evict only convicted drug-dealers. This woman, so far as I knew, was a junkie with no dealing convictions but, no doubt, along with her boyfriend and his friends, they were the main focus of drug activity on their housing estate. So where was she living now? Ammo is putting me up, she said. Ammo would never see you stuck.

There was another outburst of shouting. Somebody was selling phye. I jostled my way into the crowd. Some young men were there with lemonade bottles. The addicts were desperate. More rows. Eventually the stuff was shared out.

I spoke to one of the men selling phye. It's getting very hard to get now, he said. Sometimes the Sinn Féin is waiting outside the chemist (he named one that dispenses methadone) and they take the bottles off you and break them. That leaves us sick for the night. And what would he do with his money for selling the phye? I'm going off now to score.

Another man joined in the conversation. His face was battered and covered in dried blood. I was given a beating last night in Dolphin's Barn. And they threatened to throw us into the canal.

Was that Sinn Féin?

It was fellahs coming out the pub and they saw us. Ever since they killed Josie Dwyer there's been an awful lot of beatings in the Barn.

Josie Dwyer was the man who was kicked to death the previous year. He was an addict and reputed to be a one-time dealer. He was in late Aids. After Dwyer's death, I interviewed Alan Byrne, a man who got beaten up along with Dwyer the night that Dwyer died. Byrne lived a few doors away from Dwyer and was looking after Dwyer in the final stage of his illness. I called to Alan Byrne one morning and woke him. His was a typical junkie's flat. Needles, bloodied tissues, street phye in a lemonade bottle on the mantelpiece. What I couldn't work out was all the candle wax on top of an old telly. Was he cooking his gear by candle? No, he answered. The telly was Josie's. Josie had no electricity and we used candles for light.

I tried to imagine what it must have been like to nurse a man in late Aids in a flat with no electricity and no hot water. After Dwyer's death, one newspaper described him as a dealer who was living in "relative splendour" in his Basin Lane flat. What a stupid thing to say. There was no splendour about that flat. There's no splendour about drug addiction.

District Court, The Bridewell, Dublin;
February 1997

I had kept a note of Ashley's court appearance for her soliciting charge. I went to the Bridewell that morning and waited in Court Four. I stood just inside the door. The place was packed. Standing room only. I wondered what Ashley would look like. It was three months since I had last seen her.

It's nearly impossible to hear what's going on in the court, the buzz of talk is so loud. I pity the journalists who, on pain of being sued or done for contempt of court if they get it wrong, have to report on these proceedings. Often I can't tell what a person has been up for, it's so difficult to hear. The judge, police and legal teams talk to each other without regard to the rest of us. Justice is held in "open court" in theory only. Go along to the Bridewell any day and you'll see what I mean.

Not everyone here is facing charges. A lot of young

people come along just to see what might happen to their mates. One young man was sentenced and, as he was taken down, handcuffed to a garda, he waved a goodbye at his assembled friends, blowing kisses at the girls as he descended the steps to the cells below. The man was laughing as his friends got their last glimpse of him. Perhaps it's later in the day when the drama of the court appearance is over that the reality of the prison sentence sinks in. All your mates are out having a drink or just being free. You're stuck in the cell, same as you will be the next night and all the nights after that until you finish your sentence.

Ashley came through the door. She hugged me as she always does. It's great to see you, Paddy. She was pleased she wasn't facing court alone, she told me.

Did I imagine it or was Ashley putting on a bit of weight? Was it possible that she was off drugs?

Ashley found her brief. He took her outside to the hallway. All around, barristers were consulting with their rough, young criminal clients. Ashley's brief ran through the procedure for when her case was called. He re-assured her that nothing much could go wrong this morning. Ashley smiled at him and introduced me. He was pleased to meet me. He was a fan of my radio work. He went back into court and Ashley told me he was a good guy. I think Ashley appreciates any man who treats her decently.

Ashley's case was called. She was shaking as she stood in front of the judge and the prosecuting garda. She looked small, vulnerable. I got as close as I could. The garda was reading from his notebook. I couldn't hear what he was saying but I could make out the judge saying something about Ashley continuing her methadone maintenance programme and agreeing to see her probation officer. The judge ruled that Ashley appear again in three months.

Ashley was relieved. Outside, she asked me to come and meet Colin who was waiting around the corner in a cafe. Colin can't be seen at the court, she said, because there's too many warrants out for him.

Ashley said loads of people heard her on the radio. Her probation officer heard her and told her she was great. One of her regulars heard her, too. He was lying in bed next to his wife on a Saturday morning when he heard Ashley's voice come on the radio. His wife loved the programme. She was fascinated by Ashley and said to her husband afterwards that she couldn't understand what made some men want to be with women like that.

Colin hugged me when I met him. He bought me coffee. We're both off drugs, said Colin. We saw the film you did and we decided we don't want to live that way any more. More people should see that film. When's it going on telly?

I told Colin that I didn't know if it ever would, but there was a chance that I would get an RTE camera crew soon to make a programme with broadcast-quality equipment. I would like to talk to them both again. They said if I was doing another programme, to count them in.

We're getting married in May, they told me. We've seen the priest. You're invited to the wedding and so is Deirdre. We're going to start a new life.

St Michael's Estate, Inchicore;
April 1997

My RTE camera-crew was made available in April. The video I made with Colin and Ashley impressed enough people in RTE and it was decided that my idea for a television programme was worth a go. I would have the camera crew for just a few hours to begin with so I was determined to make the most of my chance. The night before I was due to go filming, I went looking for Ashley to see if I could get her to speak to us the next day.

It was getting dark as I walked into St Michael's. I walked towards Block Eight. Two women came out. They were linking each other, the way that whores do, in what I guess is an expression of mutual support. I got close. It was Ashley and she was in her working clothes. So she hadn't kicked her drug habit.

Hello, Ashley. Can I give you a lift somewhere?

The two of them accepted the lift to Benburb Street. Ashley was agitated. She wouldn't stop talking. Colin's in prison, she said. He won't be out until next year. They lifted him outside Pearse Street clinic when he was there looking for a de-tox. After they lifted Colin, she went back on drugs. She was just getting off the gear but when they arrested him she got so upset that she had no choice but to go back on drugs worse than ever.

Ashley said she would talk for the telly the next day. She was going to Charles Street in the morning because she was expecting to be thrown out of her squat very soon and she would need somewhere to live. I told her I would call in the morning and give her a lift into town. Ashley said she would have the place tidy in case I wanted to bring the camera crew in.

We reached Benburb Street. I left Ashley's pal out at the Smithfield end where she joined a group of four young women at the corner. Then, with Ashley, I headed downhill towards the Heuston Station end of the street. There was a dozen or more women standing by the wall of Collins's Barracks. I had never seen Benburb Street so busy. We turned up the laneway towards Arbour Hill. That's Ashley's patch.

There were more women standing there. Most of these are new, said Ashley.

I pulled the car in to let Ashley out. Mind yourself tonight, Ashley. I want you in one piece for me in the morning.

We kissed lightly and hugged strongly. Ashley wouldn't let me go. I could feel that her body was thin and slight. A junkie's body. I've seen it all before, Ashley. You junkies are always going to get off gear but you hardly ever do. You'll die soon. Like Niamh, whom I loved. Like so many others who were going to give up gear. Every junkie's like a setting sun. That how Neil Young put it in a song a long time ago.

I didn't say all this out loud, but these were my thoughts as I held Ashley in my arms. I prised her hands off me. Look after yourself tonight, Ashley. I'll see you tomorrow.

The next morning I climbed the steps of Block Eight at St Michael's. A young woman was sitting against Ashley's door, reading the *Star* and smoking. Excuse me, I said, and leaned over her to knock. You're early, she said.

She spoke with the slow, throaty voice of a junkie who had just turned on. I wondered about her comment to me about being early. Could it be that Ashley was seeing customers at her flat? If so, it was no wonder that the Corpo were evicting her. The Corpo would come under a lot of pressure from other tenants to get rid of her.

Ashley answered the door. She was just up, she said, and didn't have time yet to tidy up. Come in. I won't be able to go with you yet, Paddy, until I'm sorted. I was up in Ballymun in the middle of the night but there was no bleeding gear there. If I don't get sorted I'll be no good to you because, I don't want to be rude, but, I'll only be squeezing the cheeks of me arse together all day.

There was a lad aged about eighteen asleep on a mattress on the floor. She woke him and introduced him to me as her brother. She pushed £80 into his hand. Her last night's earnings. Get up, she said. Get downstairs and get some gear. Ashley's brother was a junkie. That's odd. My recollection from last year was that Ashley said she was the only black sheep in her family.

Ashley's brother was in a lot of pain. He had an abscess, he told me. He lifted a bandage off his left forearm. I was expecting to see something revolting but there was no obvious lesion in his skin. Rather, his arm was swollen to about twice the width it should have been and it glowed a hot, red colour. I could see the lad was ready to faint with the pain.

Ashley was impatient with her brother. Will you get up and hurry? The lad left with the money. Ashley started putting on her make-up. I can't go on the telly looking like a ghost, can I Paddy? Her hands shook and she was sweating. Excuse me, Paddy, I need the toilet. I said I would see her downstairs.

Outside I met with some of the maintenance men for the estate. They knew me. Ah, Paddy, are you here to make another radio programme? The sweet shop should be opening about now.

I looked over to where they were pointing to at Block Five. There was a group of about twenty junkies standing around, hugging themselves and shivering.

So Block Five is where it happens? I always thought Block Eight was the place for that?

Not at all, said the men. Block Five is the place we have to pick up all the silver paper. We call it the Kit Kat factory.

The junkies began to wander away again. Ashley's brother came towards me. There's no gear this morning, he said. He gave the money back to his sister who was standing beside me now. Ashley got upset. There's been a heroin shortage in

Dublin for the last two days, she said. We'll have to try Gallanstown. Can you give us a lift, Paddy?

Ashley left her brother behind and invited a man called Callow (I guess that's how you spell his name) to come with us to Gallanstown. Callow climbed into the back of my car along with his little boy. Callow is a big man. I told Callow I remembered him from eight years before when I met him in the Fettercairn estate in Tallaght. For a junkie, he was living a long time.

I mentioned the name of the man in whose house I met Callow. Ah him, said Callow. He was a nice fellah. Pity he took one turn-on too many.

No, Callow, you're wrong. Everybody in Dublin thinks that Donal is dead but he's not. (Donal is the name I will call him here. It was the name I used for him in my last book.) He's alive and well and living with his wife and children in the west of Ireland and he has kicked his heroin habit. I stayed with him and Margaret in their house out west just a few weeks ago.

Donal is a close friend of mine. I used to say to Donal, whom I have known since he was forty, that I would love to still know him when he reaches fifty, but I have never yet known a junkie to live that long. We agreed that if he lived to see fifty we would go on the beer together to celebrate. These days, I'm feeling optimistic about Donal. I think that fiftieth birthday piss-up, due in 1999, is going to happen.

As I drove out of St Michael's, a squad car started following us. He was still following us when we reached Ballyfermot. Don't worry about it, Pat, said Callow. They won't arrest you. You don't have a criminal's head on you.

I knew what he meant. Callow has criminal features. His ears and the back of his neck give him away. I don't have a criminal's head on me.

Ashley, who was in the passenger seat next to me, had her skirt hitched up and was doing something up between her legs. If they have a woman cop with them I could be strip-searched, said Ashley. I'm not letting them find my money. I had to work hard enough last night to earn it. Are you hiding your money in your knickers, Ashley? No, Paddy. I'm hiding it in me.

I turned off the Ballyfermot Road and into the housing estate of Gallanstown. The police didn't follow me. There were cops on the beat in the estate. They watched as I let Ashley and Callow out of the car. The cops didn't come near. We won't be long, said Ashley. I decided not to lose any more time. I had a camera crew waiting for me in town.

Ashley said she would see me later at Charles Street. Wait for me there, Paddy, because I really want to do this thing for the television. There's a lot I want to say.

I said goodbye and headed into town. I was already late. Cut your losses, Paddy. Don't waste any more time. Today's a new day and you'll turn up more stories that will make good TV.

I had a good day at Charles Street. It was my first day, after years of trying, that I was finally making a TV programme for broadcast. Ashley didn't show up so I never did get to put her on the telly.

A few weeks later I tried to find Ashley again, this time just to say hello. When I got to her flat in St Michael's I found the place sealed up with a heavy steel door. The Corpo had evicted her and they were stopping any more squatters from getting in. I don't know where Ashley is now.

Chapter Nine

BELFAST

Department of Social Security, Corporation Street,
North Belfast;
January 1997

The dole office here serves north Belfast which means it serves people of both religions. It's a handy spot for me to meet people whenever I want to gauge the public mood about whatever's going on. The last time I was here was the day of the publication of what was known as the Framework Document. That was during the ceasefire and it was a joint initiative of the British and Irish Governments proposing various cross-border institutions in return for which, at some point in the future, the Irish Republic would consider amending parts of its constitution with relation to Northern Ireland. I'm sorry if you think that description doesn't do justice to the Framework Document but it's the description I had to use repeatedly when, on asking people what they thought about the Document, they asked me what it was about. See if you can do better in a one-sentence description.

What I quickly learned was that people knew little about the Framework Document and cared only vaguely. The Framework Document was not a conversation-starter. For a radio vox pop to work, people have to know about and care

233

about the topic that they're being asked to comment on. Today, I would talk about things that interest people, whatever those things might turn out to be.

I saw two young men who were likely knee-cap victims. You can tell by the faces and the tattoos. They looked like criminals, or "hooods" as they say here, so they were likely to have been, at some stage, kneecapped. I walked up to them. They were smoking a joint. Very likely candidates for having their knees smashed.

I introduced myself and they were keen to talk. I was in for a crisis loan, said one. A crisis loan, I repeated, to be sure I had heard him right. Their accents were nearly impenetrable. I had to think of my radio listeners, so I repeated most of what they said. Their style of speech confirmed them as underclass young men. They would get along fine so long as they aspired to nothing more than getting the dole and drinking in the field with their mates. Beyond that limited world, they would find doors closed to them as soon as they opened their mouths.

What's the crisis?

I'm getting out of this country cos I was blamed on robbing a shap (a shop) but it was he did it. But I got the kicking.

His friend laughed and took off his baseball cap. I got a hiding too, he said, showing off cruel scars stretching from his forehead to his crown.

That's from a long time ago, said the other. We both got kickings. The last time was cos I called a Provie a wanker. The time before that, they said I was dealing drugs. I was asked to call to the Sinn Féin office to sort it out and they took me to an entrance (a laneway) and gave me one each in the knees and the elbows. They told me next time would be in the nut. And I didn't have any drink before the appointment cos I didn't know I was going to get done.

234

And were you dealing drugs?

Yes, I was. The money was great, so it was. I was getting ready to buy a car and all. But not nigh (now). This time, for the shap, I'll go over to England and let it all blow over awhile. I have mates over there.

He lifted his trouser legs. The bullet wounds were relatively clean, that is, there were neat entry and exit wounds in the calves just below the joint of the knee. He was lucky. His was a pre-ceasefire shooting. Since the ceasefire of September 1994, the IRA had increased the severity, as well as the frequency, of its attacks on young criminals. They stopped using bullets and started using concrete blocks and iron bars, like the loyalist paramilitaries do. Post-ceasefire injuries are more difficult for surgeons to repair than were pre-ceasefire ones.

The two young men told me they were attending a probation office. I would find it interesting there, they told me. Come around for a cup of tea. I took the address and thanked them and said I would try to get there over the next few days.

A man aged about twenty-five had a strange look about him. He had a long, heavy coat and a military-style haircut. His eyes had a strange intensity. He listened to me politely and attentively as I explained what I was at. He would speak to me, he said.

He was recently out of a mental hospital. It was because he had a terrible temper. He used to live with his mum but he beat her up so he had gone to live with his dad but he hit him with a frying pan. His mum's brother, home from being at sea, said he'd look after him so he got some boys to give him a kicking. They held me down and danced on my arms, he said. The next time was with baseball bats and after that, he was locked up in hospital.

Hospital was an interesting place, he said. One man there thought he was a dog. He wouldn't sleep on his bed. Only

235

under it. Another fellow thought he was a ballerina. He'd be twirling around the floor. A lot of strange people.

He gave a low whistle as he remembered the other mad people in his ward. He seemed a calm, friendly and gentlemanly sort of person. There was something about his eyes, though. I believed him when he said he had mad spells.

And how are you now?

I just attack people for no reason. I don't remember much about it afterwards. I'm on medication now. It seems to have calmed me down.

And the beating you got, was it a paramilitary thing?

The UVF. My uncle's in the UVF. What he did was for the best.

A tall man stood listening to us. You wouldn't have got the kicking if you didn't deserve it, he said. I got a kicking when I was younger. It was for robbing out of gas meters. You don't rob old people, they told me. You don't shite on your own. And they were right. I didn't do it any more. It's only assholes get a kicking. That's why most decent people support the paramilitaries.

And was it the UVF beat you?

No, it was the Provies.

Not for the first time, I noticed the high level of acceptance that there is for what's called punishment beatings, even, as in this case, by the victims themselves.

A man aged about forty with a deep voice told me he was out of work since the ceasefire ended. He was a barman and had worked in London the last twenty years. Last year he came back to Ireland and got a job in a hotel in north Antrim. Now he was too scared to stay there. There's areas he won't work in any more. I was never prejudiced, he said, but Orangemen with drink on them scare me.

I asked him what he thought about punishment beatings.

It's all wrong, he said. Who do they think they are? I got a kicking myself when I was younger. They broke my ribs.

This surprised me. He didn't look or sound like the sort of man the paramilitaries pick on.

Why were you beaten up?

They accused me of robbing the pub I worked in. They knew I didn't do it but they wanted to get me. They knew I didn't like them. They can sense that, y'know? I went to England after that. I think I'll go back there soon. There's nothing for me in this country.

It was a couple of days later that I took up the invitation I got to visit the Probation and Welfare Office around the corner. It took a bit of arranging with the bureaucracy but it was worth it.

The Probation Office trains people in metalwork, woodwork, furniture restoration and so on. There's a canteen. A tall young man who was running the canteen smiled at me as soon as I came in. 'Bout yeh, he said. (That's a Belfast greeting which, I guess, comes from, what about you? meaning how are you?). The man reminded me that I had interviewed him once coming out of the Magistrates' Court at Chichester Street. Knowing one of the young men here was a good start for me in getting the others to trust me enough to talk to me.

In the metalwork room I met a young man with a slow, clear Belfast voice. A good broadcasting voice. He put his feet up and told me his story.

I was sent here for joyriding and that. Dole fraud. Signing on in more than one place. For drugs, I got a bating. I still take drugs. Anything I can get my hands on. Ecstasy, blow, LSD.

He rolled up a trouser leg to just below the knee. His flesh was hacked and scarred.

I got spikes through my legs. The bottom of my legs. Three years ago.

What do you mean by spikes?

Baseball bats with nails in em. They pulled me out of a house, put me out the back and bate me. My mother and father was crying and all in the house but they couldn't do nothing about it. You can't do nothing about men with guns.

And this was for taking drugs?

Drug dealing. I still do it. I deal a bit of blow. There's good money in it, but it's getting very dangerous now. Then again, they can't shoot us all. There's too many doing it. The IRA shouldn't be doing that to their own people.

What do you see yourself doing when you finish your sentence?

There's good money in dealing. Blow is something everybody wants. I can't see myself giving that up.

I still think about that young man and I wonder if he will survive many more years. The IRA killed six alleged dealers during their ceasefire and greatly increased the frequency and severity of their assaults on young criminals in the Catholic community. Despite the IRA, dope-smoking is as popular as ever and raving remains one of the great cross-community activities engaged in by young people in Northern Ireland.

Occasionally, the IRA get on their moral high horse about drugs. During the ceasefire, they even went to a night-club owner and told him he'd be shot if he didn't change his music policy away from rave. I remember before the ceasefire, I was in Belfast one time when the IRA beat up sixteen young drug users and shot another one dead. Of course, the IRA's outburst of murder and assault didn't reduce drug use in Belfast, any more than it would have done anywhere else.

Paramilitary "punishments" have nothing to do with combatting drugs. Taking underclass young men out of their homes, beating them up and then putting them back again into the same environment won't stop them taking drugs.

Young people take drugs because they enjoy them. Underclass young people take drugs to excess because it's the best thrill available to them and they deal drugs because it's the most obvious way open to them to make money.

Belfast has no serious drugs problem. It has no heroin. So the drug dealing here is petty stuff. Nobody ever died from smoking dope. Sometimes people die from ecstasy use. According to one report, a total of sixteen ecstasy-users died in Ireland during the years 1992 to 1995 inclusive. I'm sceptical about that figure. I don't think that ecstasy was always the decisive factor in causing death. But it's clear that an ecstasy problem exists and a lot more needs to be done to try to reduce the dangers of ecstasy. But compared to the death toll caused through the abuse of alcoholic drink, ecstasy barely rates as a problem.

People aren't going to stop drinking, despite the death and carnage that drink causes, so there's no reason to think that they're going to stop taking ecstasy, either. Let me suggest to the IRA, if you really think you can use murder to combat social evils and improve the quality of life, then you can make a much better case for killing publicans than you can for killing Belfast drug-dealers.

I don't want you to kill publicans, either, in case you don't understand that. I just want you to stop killing and if you can't manage that, stop trying to justify murder.

Department of Social Security, Shankill Road,
Belfast;
March 1997

It was three years since I last worked the Shankill. The last time was before the ceasefires, and soon after the chip shop bomb that killed nine people. Tensions were high after that IRA bomb. I was working just around the corner from the site of the bomb blast. The gap blown out of the Shankill Road was a raw reminder of what had happened. This time, I walked up the Shankill and went past the turn for the DSS at Snugville Street, up as far as that chip shop. I found that the site has been filled by a new building under construction. I hope they put up some kind of memorial plaque there to the people who died. They have plenty of other memorials on the Shankill, in the form of garish, colourful murals listing deceased members of various UVF and UDA brigades. I hope they'll remember the civilians, too.

I took up position outside the Snugville Street DSS. If the hostility towards me was no more than last time, I would be okay. Sticks and stones etc. And I felt sure I would meet enough friendly people to be able to make my radio programme.

My first customer came out of the DSS. She was a woman aged about forty, with two small boys. Here we go. Let's see what kind of reception I was going to get.

I'm on income support, she said. I'm on my own with the children.

Do you get anything from the father of your children?

She laughed. Ah, no. He's in the big house. That's what I call it, anyhow. I used to tell the kids that daddy was in the army. We go to see him every week.

He's in prison?

She laughed again. That's right. The big house at Magherberry.

I wondered if it was to do with politics or drink. It was unlikely to be drugs because there's no heroin in Belfast and her husband would have been too old to be likely to be a raver.

May I ask you, please, what kind of offence he's in for?

He's in for rape.

She laughed again.

And has he many more years to do?

Well, he's appealing one part of the sentence. The two women told the court that since it happened that they've been having nightmares and they can't go out any more, but I've heard since that they've both been seen on the Shankill, out drinking with men.

It involved two women?

Yes. Well one was indecent assault. (She was laughing again.) But the court was very hard on him because he was convicted of that once before but I don't think he should have got so many years because it was only through drink he did it. He said it to me, even. Madge, he said, it would never have happened only for the drink. I think he went out to have an affair, but things went too far.

This woman reminded me of other rapists' wives I've met who defend and remain loyal to their husbands. In particular, she reminded me of the woman I met at the welfare in Kilkenny just two years before. As with the Kilkenny woman, I wanted this Belfast woman to say that she was well rid of her husband and wanted to get on with the rest of her life. But there seemed to be no anger in her. She just made excuses for her husband. And as with the Kilkenny woman two years before, I couldn't get past this woman's defences to find out if there was anything behind her smiling exterior. No matter what angle I tried, she kept smiling and laughing about her husband the rapist.

A couple in their forties came out. I think the woman might have been willing to speak to me but the man was abusive as soon as I told him where I was from. Get the SAS to go down south and sort out the IRA cos your government won't do it. He kept shouting stuff like that as he walked off. I think he wanted to impress the woman with him, putting the fellow from the Free State in his place. That was fine by me.

I was reminded of the last time I was here three years before when Deirdre was with me. I didn't understand what it was that a woman was shouting at me as she walked away so I just smiled and waved goodbye. Deirdre understood her, though. Did you not hear what she said? You were just told to fuck off back to the Free State or else you're a dead man.

It's true there's some not-so-nice people on the Shankill and this radio programme, like my last one, would give a slightly misleading impression of the place because it's the friendly people who end up on the air and the unfriendly ones who don't. But so long as the unfriendly ones stuck to verbal abuse I was okay. Some Catholic journalists work the Shankill by first approaching the so-called community leaders and getting their co-operation but I've never had the least interest in doing that. I don't want to hear the same old politically-approved things being said. I'll speak to whomever I like wherever I like. The DSS here at Snugville Street is my way of exploring the Shankill.

Two young men spoke with me. One of them seemed a bit simple. He was friendly and good-humoured and didn't seem to understand what I was at. The other was more serious but not unfriendly. The serious one gave me his political views. No chance of peace because neither side will give way during the marching season. The IRA is trying to take over this country, telling us where we can or can't march and we have to stand up to them. I asked this man if ever he had any Catholic friends. He answered yes. He knew many Catholics in prison. He was in prison for stealing and for not paying fines for his untaxed car.

And did you ever get in trouble with the paramilitaries for stealing?

No, he said, because it was stealing from shops in town. That's not a punishable offence. To steal from the corner shop over there would be a punishable offence. He didn't add, but it crossed my mind, that the corner shop there on the Shankill was probably also paying protection to the paramilitaries.

He used the expression "punishable offence" as if it was a recognised legal category of offence, which, here on the Shankill, in one sense it is. So-called punishment beatings are not just handed out at random, or they're not supposed to be anyway, even though in practice I have come across cases of beatings for everything from adultery to calling a paramilitary a wanker. Beatings are carried out according to a recognised code. The authority of the State has been largely supplanted here but, as in the Catholic ghettoes, it hasn't been replaced by mere anarchy; rather it's been replaced by the rule of the paramilitaries who rule according to certain customs that have at least some level of acceptance within the confines of the community. So stealing from a city centre store is okay, but stealing from the local corner shop is not.

A number of single mothers gathered around me. They all wanted flats here on the Shankill. I want to be close to my mummy.

How many times have I heard that from Dubliners who don't want to move from their home area? It's something I used to have little time for because, like most culchies, I grew up always expecting to leave my home town. What were these Dubs moaning about, having to go as far as Tallaght or whatever? Then I learned more and came to appreciate that in urban working class culture, the support of the extended family is important. When you run out of money on a Wednesday and pay day is not until the next day, it's good to have your mum close to hand. For people who don't have cars, such as young single mothers, even being a few miles in distance from your mum, say two bus journeys with a buggy and two children, is enough to leave you isolated from your family. I understand better, now, why young people on welfare, whether in Dublin or here on the Shankill, don't want to move too far from their family home.

One of the Shankill single mothers who spoke to me had been married. I have two boys, Jackie and Billy. He's named after King Billy, you know? I was away in Manchester for a couple of years but I didn't like it. My marriage broke up and I came home.

I had heard a story similar to that several times before, too. I met loads of single Protestant mums one Monday morning up the road a bit at Ballygomartin Post Office where all the women queue for income support. Lots of them had gone to England and then had come home after their marriages broke up. I knew the pattern. I took a guess and asked the young woman here on the Shankill if her ex-husband was a British soldier. He was.

The women said they wanted the ceasefire back. One had a private flat in the upstairs of a house, the gable end of which was painted with a loyalist mural. I hated them putting that there, she said, but you'd be afraid to say anything. I see the news at night and whenever there's a picture of the Shankill they always show my house with that painting on it.

The women told me that they stay out of parts of Belfast. I pointed downhill to the south where the peaceline was visible, dividing the Shankill from the Falls and the rest of Catholic west Belfast. Would you ever walk down there, down the Falls?

They laughed. Och, no. Not since the ceasefire ended. You'd get into terrible trouble, so you would.

Hold on, I said. I've walked along the Falls, just as I've walked here on the Shankill. Nobody ever bothered me.

Och, but you're fond, they said, which translates, I think, as them saying they thought I was mad.

Awhile later one of the two young men I met earlier came back, the one I thought might be a bit simple-minded. He had an older man with him. The younger man spoke to the older one. This is the fellow I was telling you about, Christopher.

Christopher was a big, bald man. He shook my hand firmly. You're from RTE? I'm pleased to meet you. And what is it you're asking about?

I had the feeling I was being checked out. I explained what I was at and Christopher said in future, he would be happy to help me if I wanted to work on the Shankill again. Just give me a call before you come. Thank you, Christopher, I said.

Christopher agreed to speak on the record. He was a taxi driver. He was out of work the last few days because his taxi was damaged by rocks thrown from a bridge while he was driving through a Catholic area. They know the Shankill black taxis, he said. One of his passengers was slightly injured. But Christopher would be okay because apart from the help he got here at the brew (the DSS), he was being looked after by the lodge.

I didn't ask what the lodge was. I could imagine Christopher in a sash and a bowler hat. He had every look of it.

A tall man in his thirties was signing on again, having just come back from Holland. I was in that country all the previous week, I told him. We swapped stories about the Irish and English pubs of Holland. Mulligans in Amsterdam, the Blue Moon in Rotterdam. He noticed, as I had done, that the pub scene in Europe had changed over the years. In the 1980s you found the Irish in the English pubs. In the 1990s you find the English in the Irish pubs. What hasn't changed is the easy friendships you find between all English-speaking men away from home.

Holland was great, he said. Like in the Blue Moon, I had plenty of mates from the Free State. Nobody ever cared, except when there's football on and we all shouted for the Irish but the Irish all shouted against the English. Then you come back to this country and it's back to the same old shite. Like my girlfriend's from Ligoniel. I'm from the Shankill but I don't want her here. It would be too dangerous. I'd rather live in a mixed area, or a Catholic area. We're going to England after we get married.

It was when I switched off my tape-recorder that his voice changed in tone. He was suddenly angry, intense, anxious. He gripped my arm and spoke in an urgent half-whisper. I can't stand this place. I hear people talk about the community spirit of the Shankill. The only community spirit here is bigotry. Who are these people to tell me who I should or shouldn't do a line with? We have our lives run by fucking paramilitaries. I hate it here. I woke up this morning just fucking depressed about facing this place again. I was born and raised here but if I never see the Shankill again it'll be too soon.

I enjoyed listening to that man. I was glad he wanted to not be part of the community. I'm sure I would feel the same in his position. That man and his fiancee were both skilled professionals, which meant that they had the ability to opt out of being part of the communities they were born into. They could sell their skills anywhere. He had no intention of sacrificing his freedom to the customs and culture of his community and its tribal leaders. By contrast, the underclass young men here accept the rule of the community. They tattoo their bodies with indelible community emblems. They never will be anything more than community members so that's what they're proud of and that's what they seek to define themselves in terms of. I would hate to be identified in that way and subjected to the customs of the community and rule of the community leaders. God preserve me from ever being a member of a community.

It began to rain. I would have to take a break from working. There was a pub across the road. I remembered the last time I was here, with Deirdre, we'd said then that if ever there was peace in Ireland, we would go in for a pint in a Shankill Road pub. The pubs here have royalist names. The Royal, the Prince This, the Princess That, The Sovereign, The Berlin Arms, for some reason. Will I go in?

Now hold on, Paddy. Even among the people of your own religion and in your own part of Ireland, you hate dealing with drunks. If there's one nasty individual in a pub, he's sure to find you. I didn't intend going around any Shankill pub with a microphone but I could be recognised by now as the fellow with the mad hat who had been standing outside the DSS the last two days asking questions. He says he's from RTE. That's Free State broadcasting.

So remember, Paddy, you hate dealing with drunks at the best of times. And remember the woman drinking in one of these places three years ago? A few thugs mistook her for a Catholic and her body turned up in a skip. She had her throat cut. With me, they wouldn't even have to make a mistake about my religion.

My imagination began to run wild. I could see myself arguing with the murder gang who would abduct me. I have no quarrel with you people. I think there should be room for both our traditions in Ireland. I could see myself saying the sort of things that many a man has said as he has gone to his death.

I think loyalist murderers are different in one respect from republican murderers. Loyalists kill you because you're from

247

the other tradition, the one they openly despise. Republicans kill you because you're from the other tradition and, through murder, republicans will bring us all together in the end to live in peace and harmony. Loyalists kill with naked sectarian bigotry. Republicans kill with sectarian bigotry clothed in layers of double-think and cant.

So, do I stay out of the Shankill's pubs until there's peace in Ireland or do I go in and have a pint? Fuck it all, there might never be peace in Ireland. It's daytime right now. Men won't be too drunk so they'll probably behave okay. Let's have a look.

Like with the pubs on the Falls, the pub I went to here on the Shankill had a sign on the door asking you to ring the bell to be allowed in. Oh fuck. That means the door will be locked again behind me. Then I realised the door was ajar. No need to ring.

The barman looked at me with curiosity but didn't seem unfriendly. I ordered a pint of Guinness. Is that a pint of Tennents, he asked? No, Guinness. Damn it, I thought, is my accent that difficult to understand?

I sat at the bar and took in my surroundings. It was a traditional Irish pub. None of your flagstones, sawdust and old junk that constitutes the "traditional" fashion of pubs in the 1990s. This pub had lino on the floor, adequate lighting and a telly with the racing on. The customers were nearly all men. There were just two women and these were middle-aged and scruffy-looking with long, greasy hair and nicotine-stained fingers. The men had the racing pages open on their newspapers.

I was surprised that there was no loyalist political paraphernalia around the walls. I was expecting this pub to be a sort of mirror-image of the nationalist pubs of the Falls or Derry's Bogside with posters and photographs and commemorative plaques for the dead. But there was nothing like that here. Not even a picture of the Queen, despite the royalist name of the pub. Over the door there was an old print of Laurel and Hardy. Around the walls there were posters advertising forthcoming musical events and a few names displayed of local winners of what we would call a raffle but which, for some reason, in Belfast, is called a ballot.

The barman gave me my pint. He was smiling and friendly. That's £1.48 please. I was quietly astonished at the price. That wasn't even two-thirds of what a pint costs in Dublin.

I opened the pages of my *Belfast Telegraph*. I knew not to bring in the *Irish News* but I realised, looking around me, that an English tabloid would have made me fit in better. I should have got the *Mirror* or the *Sun*.

I opened my newspaper. In the death columns, I saw that the same surnames appeared perhaps twenty times over. I realised that people here express their sympathy through the death columns so there are lots of notices for every death. One man, who died suddenly, was being remembered by fellow-loyalist prisoners of the Shankill. The local darts team also had a few lines to remember him. The taxi-drivers of the Shankill said he was one of the best. And there was a couple of lines from the staff and customers of the pub in which I was now sitting. We'll remember you. At my right elbow there was a large glass jar full of coins. A handwritten note on it read Loyalist Prisoners Welfare.

So I had found a similarity with the Catholic pubs. These collection boxes never say they're for raising money to kill the enemy. It's the same in the Irish pubs in New York. There's always fund-raisers for this and that prisoner's family. Why? When a man is sent to prison, his wife and family get income support. That's the same pay they would get if he was unemployed. If he did happen to have a good job before he was sent inside, then his family will suffer a drop in income and that's rough but I don't see why a prisoner's family deserve more support than any other family on social welfare. And as for the prisoners themselves, the politicals get treated better than ordinary criminals so I don't see that they need any extra help. I don't believe that the money raised in these prisoner-support campaigns goes to prisoners or their families.

I was doing the crossword in the *Telegraph* when a young man came up to me. He clapped me on the back and gave me a cheerful greeting. 'Bout yeh. Are you having any luck on the horses?

It was the fellow I referred to earlier as the simple-minded one. I realised that I had made a second mistake in trying to go incognito in this pub. Not only should I have been reading a tabloid rather than the *Telegraph,* I should have been using my biro to mark out the horses, not do the crossword. The racing page would have been the more proletarian page to be studying.

My cover was blown. This chap's a journalist from the Free State, said my simple friend. The barman, who had been regarding me with some curiosity, got up to greet me. He shook my hand. You're very welcome to the Shankill.

Awhile later, the next pint was put in front of me by a middle-aged customer. He came up and shook my hand. His face was full of happiness. Fair dues, he said, smiling. Just fair dues.

I was moved by the welcome I got. It was nice to be here and to be greeted so warmly. I left after my second pint, though. I wouldn't push my luck.